# At the Bend in the River

*An Illustrated History of Mankato and North Mankato*

*"Partners in Progress" by Ken Berg*
*Produced in cooperation with the*
*Mankato Area Chamber of Commerce*
*Windsor Publications, Inc.*
*Chatsworth, California*

# At the Bend in the River

## An Illustrated History of Mankato and North Mankato

*By Vernard E. Lundin*

Windsor Publications, Inc.—History Book Division
Managing Editor: Karen Story
Design Director: Alexander D'Anca
Photo Director: Susan L. Wells
Executive Editor: Pamela Schroeder

Staff for *At the Bend in the River:*
Manuscript Editor: Douglas P. Lathrop
Photo Editor: Patty Salkeld
Senior Editor, Corporate Biographies: Judith Hunter
Production Editor, Corporate Biographies: Albert Polito
Proofreader: Mary Jo Scharf
Customer Service Manager: Phyllis Feldman-Schroeder
Editorial Assistants: Kim Kievman, Michael Nugwynne, Michele Oakley, Kathy B. Peyser, Theresa J. Solis
Publisher's Representative, Corporate Biographies: Roxanne Landman
Layout Artist: Bonnie Felt
Designer: Ellen Ifrah

Library of Congress Cataloging-in-Publication Data
Lundin, Vernard E.
    At the bend in the river : an illustrated history of
Mankato and North Mankato / by Vernard E. Lundin. –
1st ed.
      p. 128 cm. 22 x 28
    "Produced in cooperation with the Mankato Area
Chamber of Commerce."
    Includes bibliographical references.
    ISBN 0-89781-339-1
    1. Mankato (Minn.)–History. 2. North
Mankato(Minn.)–History. 3. Mankato (Minn.)–
Description–Views. 4.North Mankato (Minn.)–Description-
-Views. 5. Mankato(Minn.)–Industries. 6. North Mankato
(Minn.)–Industries. I.Title.
F614.M2L86                  90-12247
1990776.2'1–dc20          CIP

Windsor Publications, Inc.
Elliot Martin, Chairman of the Board
James L. Fish III, Chief Operating Officer
Mac Buhler, Vice President Sponsor Acquisitions

*FRONTISPIECE: A picturesque landscape north of Mankato reveals a recently plowed corn field on a tranquil winter day. Photo by Deneve Feigh Bunde*

# Contents

# Preface

It is an honor and privilege to have been commissioned to write this history of the Mankato-North Mankato community where I have spent my entire life of more than 80 years. My most difficult problem was not in finding interesting and pertinent material but rather in deciding what would best picture the development of the community from 1852 to 1990. It would take a year or more of research and gathering material and another year to organize and write that story, which could take a thousand pages.

I regret that I have not been able to follow families from the early years, through the next two, three, and even four generations, and recognize them for their contributions. I have concentrated my efforts on industries, businesses, churches, schools, institutions, organizations, culture, public health, and recreation, all of which have contributed to the good life we enjoy today. In some instances there is a flow from one generation to another where it is important to the story.

To the many people whom I contacted for business information I apologize, because space did not permit me to include all the details provided. I am especially grateful for the help given me by Audrey Burmeister-Hicks and Mary McGrew for opening the amazingly complete archives of the Blue Earth County Historical Society to me and finding much of the material and photographs used in this book. Much of the historical flow came from the 50th, 75th, and 100th anniversary editions of the Mankato *Free Press* and other special *Progress* editions.

"The Mankato-Kasota Limestone District—A Geographical and Historic Study," a thesis compiled by Darrel F. Apitz, is a gold mine of facts for the chapter entitled "Mankato's Solid Foundation."

William Bassett, Mankato's city manager, and Robert Ringhofer, North Mankato's city administrator, have been cooperative and helpful. I also am grateful for material supplied by John Votca, director of the Mankato Technical College, and Lowell Schreyer of the Mankato State University News Bureau.

*The turning leaves of autumn add splashes of warmth to the verdant countryside. Photo by Joe Miller*

# The Bend in the River

More than a million years ago, the townsite of Mankato was buried deep under hundreds of feet of ice during the first of four glacial periods which geologists call the Great Ice Age. As the glaciers advanced and receded over a span of about two million years, they created the geologic and geographic features of Minnesota and much of North America as well. By their tremendous and relentless grinding, gouging, and shoving of the earth, the glaciers left areas of fertile, sandy soil; exposed regions of granite, limestone, and iron ore; and created rivers, lakes, swamps, hills, and valleys.

During the last of the four glacial periods, a period called the Wisconsin Age, the ice reached as far south as Des Moines, Iowa. As the climate warmed, melting ice from the tremendous glacier formed a huge lake that covered the northwestern part of Minnesota, the Red River Valley, and parts of North Dakota and Canada. Waters from this inland sea, named Lake Agassiz, poured southeastward in a vast flow called the River Warren. By some force of nature which geologists cannot explain, this mighty stream formed a sharp bend at the site of what is now Mankato and flowed northward to join the Mississippi at St. Paul.

Centuries later, as the floods receded and the land dried out, Indians moved into the area, traveling up and down the river by canoe. Some camped at or near the great bend. European ex-

plorers followed those same waterways in search of the mythic Northwest Passage to the Far East. Like the Indians before them, the explorers used the St. Lawrence River and the Great Lakes as their passage into the vast interior, including what is now Minnesota.

It was not until 1700, however, that one of these European explorers paid particular attention to the area that would become Mankato. That year a Frenchman named Pierre Le Sueur, who had been on several previous expeditions into Minnesota, returned to search for copper. On one of his earlier trips he had observed Sioux Indians using a blue-green clay for war paint, and from its color he believed it to be rich in copper. He learned that the colored soil came from deposits near the big bend of the Minnesota River, then called St. Pierre's by the French and later St. Peter's by the British.

Le Sueur and his party arrived at the bend of the Minnesota River in October, after a hard trip by boat and canoe up the Mississippi River from Biloxi. The group moved on to the tributary stream called Mahkato, or "blue earth," by the Indians. Just a short distance, upstream Le Sueur observed the blue soil he sought in banks along the river.

Because winter was approaching, Le Sueur first built several rough cabins for shelter and erected a stockade of logs for protection. He named the place Fort L'Huillier for a French official who had assisted him in outfitting his expedition. Settlers later simplified the name to LeHiller. An unincorporated suburb of Mankato later took on that name.

Le Sueur's men spent the winter mining the blue soil and in the spring loaded about two tons of it into a boat for transportation to France. There are no records to show that it ever arrived. Nothing was lost, however, as the questionable "ore" later was assayed as worthless blue clay. The intrepid Frenchman did acquire a bit of wealth of another kind. He had brought with him a large supply of goods that he knew were popular with the Indians, and through that trade he accumulated many beaver pelts. Le Sueur's expedition left permanent reminders of his visit to the bend of the river. The stream where his visions of rich copper ore turned to blue clay was named the Blue Earth, and Mankato is the seat of Blue Earth County. Le Sueur's name was given to a city about 20 miles from the mouth of the Blue Earth, as well as a river and a county.

After the Revolutionary War the newly born United States of America, by the Treaty of Paris of 1783, gained that part of Minnesota east of the Mississippi. By the Louisiana Purchase in 1803 the United States secured from France that part of Minnesota west of the Mississippi. After the War of 1812 the British relinquished their interest in the remainder of the upper Mississippi

Valley and the British period in the Upper Midwest ended.

To secure the newly gained territory and encourage the nation's growth, the government established Fort Snelling in 1819 on a bluff overlooking the junction of the Minnesota and Mississippi rivers. A few years later, in 1825, the government negotiated with the Sioux and Chippewa tribes, archenemies for generations, to establish a boundary line between them. That line extended roughly from Chippewa Falls in Wisconsin, zigzagging across what is now Minnesota to the Red River at a point near present-day Moorhead. This boundary line, never really observed by the Indians, became an important factor in later treaties.

By purchase from the Sioux and Chippewa, the government obtained about 5,000 square miles of land between the upper Mississippi and St. Croix rivers which became vital to Minnesota's development. The first three towns in Minnesota—St. Paul, St. Anthony, and Stillwater—were founded between 1838 and 1845. In 1848 Congress created the Minnesota Territory and rapid population growth followed. Hardy pioneers, who were actually squatters on Indian lands, moved into the Minnesota Valley. Alexander Ramsey, who had been appointed governor of the Minnesota Territory, understood that his first important task in the nation's expansion movement was to acquire the "Suland," the name given

*Chief Sleepy Eye (Esh-ta-hum-bah), depicted here in a painting by Henry Inman, had his tribal village near the bend of the river before the white men came. When reservations were established after the Treaty of Traverse des Sioux, Sleepy Eye asked that the area his people occupied be included in a reservation. He yielded, however, when he was given two barrels of pork and other gifts. Courtesy, Minnesota Historical Society*

*BELOW: In 1852, Henry Jackson, cofounder of Mankato, formed a townsite company to secure funds needed to develop the newly founded city. Although he longed to see the city grow, he did not live long enough to see his dreams materialize. Courtesy, Blue Earth County Historical Society*

*BELOW RIGHT: Parsons K. Johnson, depicted here, and Henry Jackson of St. Paul were the original settlers of Mankato. In 1850 the two men made an excursion up the Minnesota River by steamboat and were impressed by the beauty and fertility of the land around the bend of the river. In 1852 Johnson staked out a townsite and then continued to take an active role in developing the settlement. Courtesy, Blue Earth County Historical Society*

to southern Minnesota by traders, early settlers, and frontier newspapers.

Working with Commissioner of Indian Affairs Luke Lea, Governor Ramsey in July 1851 summoned the Upper Sioux tribes, the Sisseton and Wahpeton, to a conference at Traverse des Sioux ("crossing of the Sioux"), about 12 miles downstream from the big bend of the Minnesota River. For 10 days, as the Sisseton and Wahpeton arrived, there were games, feasts, and plenty of firewater to drink. On July 23 the tribal chiefs signed a treaty ceding their part of the Suland south of the 1825 treaty line. For this vast empire, U.S. government agents agreed to pay the Indians more than $1.6 million in cash and annuities. The agents also secured the chiefs' names on another document which said that debts owed to traders by individual Indians would be taken off the top of tribal payments. This bit of trickery would prove to be a factor in the Sioux uprising a few years later. From Traverse des Sioux, Ramsey and Lea went back down the river to Mendota where they negotiated a sim-

ilar treaty with the Lower Sioux tribes, the Mdewakanton and the Wahpekute. Ceded to the government for $1.4 million in cash and annuities was an area including the southeast quarter of what became Minnesota.

As part of the Traverse des Sioux treaty, the Upper Sioux agreed to move to a reservation that covered 10 miles on each side of the Minnesota River from its headwaters at Big Stone Lake to the Yellow Medicine River near present-day Granite Falls. The Lower Sioux agreed to a strip of the same width along the Minnesota from the Yellow Medicine River to Little Rock Creek north of Sleepy Eye. Even before the treaties were signed in Washington and the Sioux could get to the reservations, settlers were moving into the territory the Indians had signed away.

It was cheap land that drew the adventurous to Suland. Under the U.S. government's Pre-Emption Act of 1841, district land offices sold surveyed land for a minimum of $1.25 an acre, and those who moved into land not yet surveyed were given the option to purchase their claims later. In newly acquired territories the government reserved sections of land for the development of railroads, schools, and universities, and this land too was sold, sometimes at prices even lower than the district land offices offered. The flow of pioneers, many recruited from northern European countries, increased sharply when free land was offered under the

*LEFT: Mrs. Johnson was one of the earliest permanent settlers of Mankato, arriving in 1852. She played a major role in helping her husband, Parsons K. Johnson, build the city. Courtesy, Blue Earth County Historical Society*

*RIGHT: Mrs. Jackson was one of the first residents of Mankato. Her husband founder Henry Jackson, died at an early age. She later married John S. Hinckley, another early settler who donated land for the log cabin school. Courtesy, Blue Earth County Historical Society*

Homestead Act of 1862.

Sensing that the flow of early settlers would require service centers, entrepreneurs sought advantageous locations for townsites. Among them were Parsons K. Johnson and Henry Jackson of St. Paul. They had made an excursion on a steamboat, the *Anthony Wayne,* up the Minnesota River in 1850 and were impressed by the beauty and fertility of the land around the bend of the river. Johnson probably had heard of the Minnesota River Valley from his mother, a granddaughter of Jonathon Carver, an early British explorer and mapmaker.

With two friends, Daniel Williams and W. W. Paddock, Johnson and Jackson started up the frozen Minnesota River by cutter and sleigh in February 1852. Jackson became ill and had to return to St. Paul. But Johnson made it to the bend of the river and staked out a townsite, and on returning to St. Paul he and Jackson formed a townsite company to secure funds they needed to develop a city. Others in the company were Colonel D.A. Robertson,

Samuel Leech, J.C. Ramsey, J.M. Castner, J.S. Hinckley, D.F. Brawley, Robert Kennedy, and William Hartshorn.

At a meeting in St. Paul, company members pondered over a name for their town. Johnson City was suggested but vetoed by Johnson himself. Reaching no conclusion, they called in two sisters, Laura Johnson and Angeline Jackson Bivens, to give the envisioned town a name.

Someone recalled the writings of Joseph Nicollet, who stated that the country at the bend of the river reminded him of the legendary Undine region in Germany–a land of lakes, rivers, and waterfalls, ruled over by a nymph called Mahkato. According to local legend, Nicollet confused the name of a Sioux chief, Mankato, with the name of the nymph and when his journals were printed Mahkato became Mankato. Whatever the origins of the name, the Johnson and Jackson wives said Mankato was good enough for them, and thus the new town at the bend of the river got its name.

*After the arrival of the first railroad in 1868, there were few steamboats on the Minnesota River. However, excursion boats continued to paddle upstream from St. Paul. A popular boat was the* Henrietta, *shown here at the Mankato levee on May 4, 1897. Courtesy, Blue Earth County Historical Society*

# A City Is Born

Parsons K. Johnson and Henry Jackson wasted no time getting back to Mankato after the first exploratory trip. Their first act was to build lean-to shelters, using saplings and brush, to establish their own claims. Later, in the spring of 1852, Johnson erected the first house, a 12-by-12-foot log cabin. Jackson soon followed with a second cabin, and a man known only as General Robinson built a log building and opened a general store, hiring Evans Goodrich to run the business for him.

A steam paddle wheeler, the *Tiger,* churned up the Minnesota River that spring with the first settlers and made two more trips from St. Paul that season. The first white woman to settle in Mankato, Mrs. James Rabin, arrived on the *Tiger*'s second trip on April 29. Another steamboat, the *Black Hawk,* also made three trips to Mankato in 1852, bringing more home seekers and supplies needed at the settlement.

The new town took time to celebrate the Fourth of July and took further time off on July 5 when the *Black Hawk* berthed at the Mankato landing with 40 passengers. Fifteen of those travelers remained in Mankato, while the rest pressed farther up the Minnesota Valley. Thus, in its first year the infant city became the head of river traffic, the gateway to the wilderness of the Upper Minnesota Valley and the vast prairielands extending into what would become the Dakota Territory. Private homes opened their doors to the new arrivals and served as temporary rooming houses. But soon buildings designed strictly as hotels began to appear. The first to open was the Mankato City Hotel, which was actually just outside the city boundary.

In December 1852 the Mankato Townsite Company arranged for the construction of the first legitimate hotel, envisioned as a large two-story frame structure. This hotel, which was to be called the Mankato House, stood at the site of what later became the corner of Hickory and Front streets.

General Samuel Leech, supervisor of the hotel project, became ill and had to return to St. Paul for treatment, leaving the hotel unfinished. The townsite company then sold the two lots and the framework to Henry Shaubut, who finished the 32-by-50-foot structure by adding a wing to house his family. The second floor was left open as one big room, which served as a dormitory for stagecoach drivers, teamsters, and overflow hotel guests. The Mankato House became a community center for business and social events and, with additions and remodeling, served as the leading hotel until 1890, when it was converted into a clothing store.

Another pioneer log hotel was the Minnesota House, built by a German immigrant, Clements Kron, who also operated a livery stable adjacent to his hotel. After Kron's death his daughter and son-in-law, Anna and Joseph Stahl, replaced the log building with a frame

*Mankato's first hotel, the Mankato House, was built with lumber carried by steamboat from St. Paul. It was finished in 1854 and became the community center for business and social gatherings. Located at the corner of Front and Hickory streets, it stood until 1890 when it became a clothing store. It later became the site of the National Citizens Bank which still stands as the Matt J. Graif building. Courtesy, Blue Earth County Historical Society*

structure. This building, in turn, was moved off the site to make way for a three-story brick hotel named the Stahl House. This hotel operated continuously until 1983, when it was converted into a month-to-month boardinghouse. Still other hotels of the early Mankato period included the Washington House at Main and Second streets, the Union Hotel on North Front Street, the Minneopa House in South Bend, and the Clifton House on South Front Street.

Steamboats continued the St. Paul-Mankato service for several years, operating whenever the river was deep enough to navigate. The river was unpredictable and was passable in some years only for a brief time following the spring thaw. The *Black Hawk* made regular trips in 1853, but the river was too low for travel in 1854. Only one boat, the *Globe,* made the Mankato landing that year, on May 20. There were 109 steamboat arrivals recorded in 1855, 207 in 1856, and 310 in 1858, the peak year. J.J. Shaubut, brother of Henry Shaubut, acted as the agent for all of the steamboats coming to the Mankato landing, and his store was an active and

popular place. Shaubut operated a warehouse near the store and another at the landing, from which he shipped out grain and other products from the pioneer farmers of the area.

River traffic fell off rapidly after the banner year as roads were developed. Two of the larger vessels, the *City Belle* and the *Fanny Harris,* made regularly scheduled trips in 1861. In 1862 the *Favorite* claimed a record by making the St. Paul-to-Mankato upstream trip in 19 hours and the return trip downstream to St. Paul in 12 hours.

The years of the steamboat boom brought significant growth and permanent development in Mankato and its environs. The Minnesota Territorial Legislature created Blue Earth County in 1853 with Mankato as the county seat. On April 14 the first recorded deed to property in the county went to Edwin Perkins of St. Paul. He was registrar of deeds, but after two months in office Perkins decided he did not want to move to Mankato so he resigned. He was succeeded by the capable and respected Parsons K. Johnson, who had been appointed Mankato's first postmaster by President Franklin Pierce. Johnson also served as justice of the peace and was elected to the state legislature, where he served for 14 consecutive years.

Building roads was difficult in the untamed Minnesota Territory, with streams to cross, swamps and lakes to avoid, and trees to fell, but in 1853 a crude military road connected Mankato with St. Paul. Another road was opened between Mankato and Read's Landing on the Mississippi at the shore of Lake Pepin. Soon stagecoach lines sprang up to meet the need for more dependable mail and passenger service than steam-

LEFT and BELOW: For many years, four hotels— the Ben Pay, the Saulpaugh, the Stahl House, and the Burton— provided adequate rooms for salesmen, travelers, and visitors. All have been replaced by motor inns and motels. Only the oldest, the Stahl House, still stands at the corner of Front and Plum streets but is now a rooming house for low-income residents. The Ben Pay, below, was razed to make room for a parking ramp and a park. The venerable Saulpaugh, left, which was the popular choice for business meetings and social affairs also came down under urban renewal, and a spacious Holiday Inn was constructed on the site. Courtesy, Blue Earth County Historical Society

boats could provide.

George H. Marsh, who had opened a Mankato general store with his brother in 1854, secured a government contract to pick up the mail every week from Fort Snelling. His first run from Mankato in reality was a walk— Marsh went on foot to Traverse des Sioux and there hired an Indian to paddle him by canoe to the fort. For the return trip he secured a light rig and a horse. Before long he went to a two-horse team and a rig large enough to carry a passenger or two. By the summer of 1856 mail and passenger service was available three times a week. Additional stagecoach companies were formed and started routes that went in all directions from Mankato. Four-horse teams were used on main routes and relay stations were established. By changing horses at the relay stations, a stagecoach could make the trip from Mankato to St. Paul in a single day.

With the coming of railroads that extended lines to even small towns, the stagecoaches faded from the Minnesota scene. The demise of the stagecoach marked the beginning of the end for two fledgling settlements near Mankato. Mankato City, laid out on the stone prairie just north of the original Mankato plat, and South Bend, a settlement about a mile across the Blue Earth River, were out of position for steamboats and later railroads. Boosters in these two settlements finally gave up the battle and their dreams.

The opening of new businesses and industries in Mankato, however,

*The Clifton House, a pioneer hostelry, was the last survivor of the several wood structures on Front Street. It stood until 1930 when it was demolished to make way for an office building for the Northern States Power Company. That building, too, fell before the needs of urban renewal and the site is now a parking lot. Courtesy, Blue Earth County Historical Society*

continued steadily through the 1850s and 1860s. The first blacksmith shop in Mankato and Blue Earth County was started in 1853 by Joseph Keene. The first school, supported by public subscription, opened in the same year with 24 pupils and Sarah Jane Hanna as the teacher. The first government survey of the land at the bend of the river was made in 1854. There were no benchmarks, so the surveyors pounded their key stake at what became the corner of Front and Main streets. As a result of the survey, many parcels claimed by the early settlers had to be altered, with some people gaining and others losing.

Leo Lamm posted signs for his boot and shoe store in 1853. Two wagon and carriage manufacturers opened shops. Sawmills began turning logs into lumber, and limestone quarries and lime kilns began production. A

small flour mill began grinding wheat. A furniture factory added comfort and convenience to log cabin homes. The *Independent,* Mankato's first newspaper, published its first issue on July 13, 1857. The *Mankato Record* began publication two years later. William Bierbauer started the first brewery in 1857 and in a few years there were eight more. But only the Bierbauer Brewery, at the head of Rock Street, was still making beer when the Prohibition Amendment went into effect in 1920. The plant stood idle until Prohibition was repealed in 1933 and it then resumed production for several years. Finally, Bierbauer's went the way of hundreds of small local breweries throughout the country and closed its doors permanently. By the 1980s nothing remained of the impressive landmark perched on the bluff overlooking the bend of the river.

Although the people of Mankato felt quite secure after the Sioux tribes were moved to their reservations in 1853 and the United States government established Fort Ridgely in the Minnesota Valley, minor incidents did cause uneasiness. The fears intensified in 1857 when an outlaw Wahpekute chief, Inkpaduta, and a small band of Lower Sioux renegades went on a rampage and murdered 30 white settlers at Lake Okoboji in northwest Iowa. After that incident, called the Spirit Lake Massacre, Inkpaduta moved north to Jackson County in Minnesota, where he and his men killed several more settlers. Learning of the killings, the Department of Indian Affairs in Washington, D.C., requested federal troops to hunt down the renegades; but they had already fled. Chief Little Crow was coerced into organizing a posse of reservation Indians, but this pursuit also proved fruitless. Indians on the reservations resented the failure of the "great white father" to track down the outlaws and were further incensed when the

Washington bureau announced that no more annuities would be paid until Inkpaduta was captured and brought to justice.

Even though the punitive action was recalled, the whole affair was another straw the Indians could add to their bundle of grievances. Tensions on the reservations reached the breaking point in 1862 after a crop failure and a winter of near-starvation. When annuity

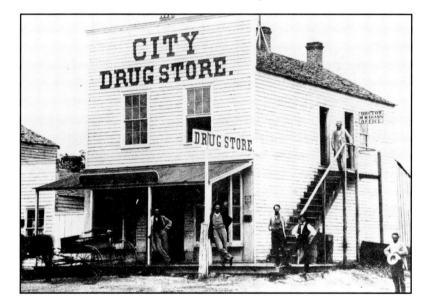

*BELOW: As the newly found city of Mankato began to grow, new businesses sprang up to serve the needs of the residents. One such business was the City Drug Store, depicted here in the 1860s. This establishment also housed the medical office of Dr. Mahan. Courtesy, Blue Earth County Historical Society*

*LEFT: The opening of new businesses in Mankato flourished in the second half of the nineteenth century. Depicted in this 1880s image is the R. J. Thomas grocery store. Located on Front Street, the store supplied customers with an array of goods including bulk beans and other important staples. Courtesy, Blue Earth County Historical Society*

*Before the Dakota Sioux had signed away their land with the Traverse des Sioux Treaty, they inhabited the wilderness that was to become Mankato. This scene depicts Minneopa Falls, which is now part of Minneopa State Park, one of the oldest state parks in Minnesota. In the Dakota Sioux language Minneopa means "twice-falling waters," referring to the two waterfalls in the park. Courtesy, Blue Earth County Historical Society*

payments from Washington failed to arrive when due in late June or early July, the hungry Indians on the upper Sioux reservation demanded food from stocks in the agency's warehouse which, they claimed, rightly belonged to them. Usually the government agent distributed annuity money and food supplies at the same time and adamantly held to that policy. Under great pressure, however, he relented and issued some food. This bought time and temporary calm. Early in August Chief Little Crow was promised additional food for his people, but the promise was never kept, nor would the agent extend credit until the annuities arrived.

The spark that touched off the bloody Sioux Uprising was ignited in Meeker County on a hot day in August 1862. Four young Indians were returning to their reservation after a hunting trip when they found a hen's nest at a farm near Acton. A dispute erupted over whether to take the eggs. One Indian called his companion a coward, afraid to take a white man's egg even while he was half-starved. The accused said he was not afraid and would go kill a white man to prove it.

The four Indians then went to the farmhouse and asked the homesteader, Robinson Jones, for liquor. Jones refused and soon took off to join his wife at the home of their neighbor, Howard Baker. There the Indians challenged Jones, Baker, and another neighbor, Veranus Webster, to a "friendly" shooting match. As the Indians emptied their guns into the target, they were quick to reload. Because the three white men failed to follow suit, they were helpless and were murdered on the spot. The Indians also killed Mrs. Jones, but Mrs. Baker and Mrs.

Webster escaped by hiding. The four young braves then returned to the Joneses' place, where they killed an adopted daughter named Clara Wilson.

When word of the Acton massacre got back to the reservation, the tribal chiefs decided that the time had come to attack the whites. They persuaded Little Crow to lead the assault, feeling he alone had the prestige and skill to unite the tribes. Historians believe that Little Crow accepted the challenge despite his belief that the Sioux could never win an all-out war against the swarm of white settlers.

On August 18, the day after the Acton murders, the Sioux attacked the government agencies at both the upper and lower reservations and ambushed a company of soldiers trying to cross the river at the Redwood ferry, killing 24 of the troopers. Bands of Indians raided settlements in the valley and isolated farm families. Word of the rampaging Indians spread quickly, and terrified settlers fled to New Ulm for safety. Some refugees also made their escape to Mankato, which had organized a makeshift militia to hold off the expected assault. That assault never materialized, but twice the Sioux descended on New Ulm and twice on Fort Ridgely.

When a rider from Fort Ridgely reached St. Paul to report the Indian attacks, Governor Alexander Ramsey commissioned his friend, Henry H. Sibley, to relieve Fort Ridgely and subdue

*ABOVE: Chief Little Crow led the Dakota Sioux uprising in 1862 and fled into the Dakota territory after his forces were defeated in battle at Wood Lake. On a foraging trip back into Minnesota in 1863, he was shot and killed near Hutchinson while picking berries with his 16-year-old son. Courtesy, Blue Earth County Historical Society*

*Henry Hastings Sibley, Minnesota's first governor, was the territorial manager for the American Fur Company. He established a trading post at what is now Sibley Park before Johnson and Jackson started the Mankato settlement. Sibley was commissioned as a colonel by Governor Alexander Ramsey and was authorized to raise an armed force to put down the Sioux uprising in 1862. His militia of make-shift soliders marched to the relief of New Ulm and Fort Ridgely and won the battle of Wood Lake, which was the last of the Indian war. Courtesy, Minnesota Historical Society*

the hostiles. "Colonel" Sibley had no formal military training, but he knew the Sioux and their language and customs from his contacts with them as a fur trader.

Only raw recruits, who had little training and even less equipment, were available to Sibley. Many of Minnesota's had boldly answered the call to join the Union forces in the Civil War. Still, Sibley, with an army of 1,600, relieved Fort Ridgely on August 27. With Fort Ridgely secure, Sibley's troops took the offensive. After Sibley's command arrived, a decisive battle was waged at Birch Coulee. Thirteen white men were killed and 40 seriously wounded. Survivors lay behind dozens of horses that had been killed by the Indians. Reinforced by a few trained soldiers, more guns and ammunition, and more horse-drawn wagons with supplies, the troops engaged the Indians in several skirmishes and finally won a decisive victory at Wood Lake.

The Wood Lake defeat ended all organized Sioux resistance and Little Crow retreated, leaving his prisoners

with Indians who were friendly to the whites. Within a few days 107 white captives and 162 more of mixed blood were turned over to Colonel Sibley at a place near the present-day city of Montevideo. Sibley named the site Camp Release and a 51-foot granite shaft was put up there as a monument to the end of the Sioux uprising. Some of the Sioux warriors who had taken part in the uprising fled into the Dakota Territory and others were taken prisoner by the military. A five-man military commission was quickly appointed to try the Indians for their crimes. The commission met at Camp Release on September 28, but the Indian trials did not begin until October 25, because it took Sibley some time to move his captives to the Lower Sioux Agency. On some days the commission paraded as many as 40 Indians before the board. Some captives were heard and tried in five minutes or less. In what many students of the uprising term a travesty of justice, 307 Indians were sentenced to death and 16 others to prison terms.

General John Pope, a Union officer in the Civil War, and Colonel Sibley favored immediate execution, but because of the vast number of capital cases, permission was sought from the President of the United States. General Pope telegraphed the final list of 307 condemned Indians to President Lincoln. The frugal president, by mail, (General Pope's telegram had cost $400) ordered the general to send the complete record of each convict. He authorized deputies to study the trial papers and to distinguish between murderers and rapists and those who had only been participants in battle.

While the records were being studied in Washington, Sibley marched about 1,700 Sioux men, women, and children to Fort Snelling, where they were confined in a fenced compound along the Minnesota River. Then he moved the 307 condemned to die to Camp Lincoln, just outside of Mankato. During the night of December 4, a mob of vengeful Mankato citizens intent on slaying the condemned men moved across the Blue Earth River, but they were turned back by soldiers stationed there as guards. On the following day the prisoners were moved to safer quarters within Mankato itself.

On December 6, 1862, President Lincoln approved the death sentence for only 39 of the 307, and personally wrote on executive mansion stationery the names of those to be hanged. He said the executions should take place December 19, but then agreed to a week's delay to permit more time for arrangements. Missionaries spent much time with those condemned to die and a number of baptisms took place. One Indian got a last-minute reprieve when a final review showed that his only accusers were two small boys.

Early in the morning of December 26, the 38 convicts began chanting their death songs, which continued until they were taken at 10 o'clock to the gallows that had been set up in a public square. About 1,400 soldiers formed solid lines around the platform to keep order among the hundreds of curious citizens who thronged around the square.

Nooses were placed around the necks of the 38, who all stood on a single platform. Given the signal, an axe man with one swing severed the retaining rope and the platform dropped, leaving the 38 dangling until they were dead. Witnesses gave only a muffled cry as the platform dropped and then

stood in silent awe as the largest mass execution in United States history was carried out.

The Sioux were banished from Minnesota after the 1862 uprising, though some returned later to live peaceably on small reserves. But with the Indian threat eliminated and former reservation land available for sale, hundreds of settlers poured through Mankato to stake their future in the Minnesota Valley. Mankato grew steadily, and when the first official U.S. census was taken in 1860, its population numbered 1,561. A state census taken in 1865 raised that number to 1,973.

There was great excitement in Mankato on May 20, 1867, when the steamboat *Julia*, risking a trip from St. Paul in spite of low water, hit a snag about a mile below the Mankato landing and sank. The town was almost deserted as everyone turned out to see the wreck. The vessel did not completely submerge, not a single passenger was lost or injured, and even some of the cargo was salvaged. The sunken hull was visible in the river until ice floes and spring floods tore it apart, erasing all evidence of the only steamboat lost in Mankato's history.

A boom began after the arrival in Mankato of the first train over the Minnesota Valley Railroad (also called the St. Paul and Sioux City Railroad) on October 3, 1868. That train had only a few freight cars. The roadbed needed further leveling before passenger service was inaugurated on October 12. By then timetables listed the arrival and departure of two trains each day.

October 20 was the day set to celebrate the coming of the railroad. On that morning the depot platform was thronged with people to see the arrival

DAKOTA (SIOUX) MEMORIAL - 1862

The last act of Minnesota's Dakota (Sioux) War took place here in Mankato on December 26, 1862, when thirty-eight Dakota Indians died in a mass execution on this site.

The Dakota War was a culmination of years of friction between Dakota and white as settlement pushed into Indian hunting grounds. Government agents and missionaries hoped the Dakota could be taught to live as farmers and worship as Christians, but, as Chief Big Eagle said many years later, "it seemed too sudden to make such a change.... If the Indians had tried to make the whites live like them, the whites would have resisted, and it was the same way with many Indians." The Minnesota uprising was one of the nation's most costly Indian wars, both in lives lost and property destroyed. It resulted in the near depopulation of the frontier and the exile of the Dakota from Minnesota.

At the war's conclusion, several hundred Indian prisoners were tried by a five-man military commission, and on November 5, 1862, 303 were condemned to death. Henry B. Whipple, Episcopal bishop of Minnesota, talked with President Abraham Lincoln on behalf of the Indians. After listening to the bishop and personally reviewing the trial records, Lincoln commuted the death sentence for all but thirty-eight prisoners.

At 10 a.m. on December 26, 1862, the condemned men, chanting the Dakota death song, marched in single file to a scaffold guarded by 1,400 troops in full battle dress. A crowd of citizens was on hand to witness the largest mass execution in United States hist...

*ABOVE: Chief Amos Owen of the Prairie Island Mdewakanton Dakota Sioux conducted a memorial service for the 38 Indians who were executed at the site of this marker on December 26, 1862. Invoking the spirits of the four winds with his pipestone peace pipe, he called the roll of the 38 with their Indian names. Photo by John Cross*

*FACING, TOP: On October 20, 1868, the first train arrived in Mankato bringing with it a new era in transportation. Depicted here in 1917 is a cheerful crowd at the Union depot seeing off World War I soldiers. Courtesy, Blue Earth County Historical Society*

of a special train with 500 passengers from St. Paul. The expected dignitaries included ex-governor Alexander Ramsey; Henry Sibley, who had served as the first governor of Minnesota, which gained statehood in 1858; Mayor Steward of St. Paul; Colonel Merriam; and Edmund Rice, who was generally recognized as the father of railroads in Minnesota.

The Mankato band and a Minnesota Valley Railroad band headed a procession of more than 1,000 people from the depot on Fourth Street to the new brick Burr building, where a sumptuous dinner had been prepared by the nearby Clifton House staff. The *Mankato Record,* reporting on the day's activities, meticulously listed foods on the menu.

The crowd feasted, the *Record* said, on "50 turkeys, 10 geese, 20 ducks, 100 chickens, 15 tongues, and 12 hams, making a total of 1,170 pounds of meat; 310 pies, 50 large frosted cakes, 25 plain cakes, and 12 jelly cakes." Other items listed included celery, sardines, jelly, pickles, fritters, small cakes, cheese, catsup, coleslaw, and three barrels of coffee. The day after the railroad celebration, there was another important "first." The depot agent received the first message over the just completed telegraph line and Mankato could finally enjoy almost instant communication with the outside world.

To return the favors received at Mankato, St. Paul officials invited Mankato dignitaries and businessmen to visit their city on October 29. The Minnesota Valley Railroad provided 200 tickets for the Mankato party.

The completion of the Winona and St. Peter Railroad in 1871 gave

Mankato another route to market for farmers of the area. The Minnesota Valley Railroad eventually became the Chicago, St. Paul, Minneapolis and Omaha line, and the Winona and St. Peter became part of the Chicago and North Western system. Within a few years the Chicago, Milwaukee, St. Paul and Pacific Railroad and the Chicago Great Western both extended lines to Mankato, and the Minneapolis, Northfield and Southern ran a passenger service from Faribault to Mankato over the Great Western tracks. Soon Mankato became the hub for railroads that served all of southern Minnesota.

## A Monumental Battle

In 1902, 40 years after the Sioux War, still-vengeful Mankato citizens raised funds to buy a large granite monument, which was erected on the site of the famous Indian execution. In bold relief the inscription stated simply, "Here Were Hanged 38 Sioux Indians December 26, 1862."

The monument stood for more than 70 years before it was removed to make way for urban renewal. Still, there were some who insisted that the monument should be relocated and preserved for its historical significance. Others objected to the original inscription, which they considered arrogant and demeaning.

As Mankato's mayor at that time, the author appointed a committee to recommend a suitable replacement. Theodore L. Nydahl, an historian himself, was selected to write an account of the reasons be-

hind the uprising that would be accepted by the Sioux then residing in Minnesota. In 1976 the project became a high priority for the Mankato Bicentennial Commission. The Minnesota Historical Society offered to donate a bronze plaque, which was mounted on a stone marker secured by George Weckman. The new marker was placed in a small parquette adjoining the Minnesota Valley Regional Library, very close to the actual execution site. At dedication ceremonies, Chief Amos Owen of the Mdewakanton band conducted a memorial service for the 38 Sioux who were hanged.

In 1987, which Governor Rudy Perpich proclaimed a Year of Reconciliation, the parquette was further enhanced by a striking, life-sized bust of an Indian in his bonnet, sculpted from a block of Mankato limestone by Thomas Meagher Miller, a local artist. This

*This massive stone memorial chiseled from a block of Mankato limestone by local sculptor Thomas Meagher Miller stands on the site of the 1862 Sioux executions. Courtesy, City of Mankato*

statue now stands beside the memorial marker. A flagstone walk and stone benches provide a quiet place for rest and contemplation.

*The Cummings ferry, operating near Sibley Park, was one of two which crossed the Minnesota River from Mankato to North Mankato before the iron bridge was built in 1879. Courtesy, Blue Earth County Historical Society*

# Two Cities Hand in Hand

**W**hen Mankato received its city charter from the Minnesota legislature on March 6, 1868, the town was already the key city of southern Minnesota. Since its founding in 1852, Mankato citizens had been left pretty much to their own devices, the village fathers imposing few regulations and restrictions on their freewheeling frontier life-style. A glimpse into that way of life is available in the 1868 charter, as well as a hint of the changes to come.

Mankato's first government was to consist of a mayor, treasurer, recorder, two justices of the peace—all elected by the citizens at large—and three councilmen elected from each of three wards. One of the first charges of these new officers would be to remove the remaining vestiges of the frontier era. For example, the charter outlawed "immoderate driving or riding in the streets," and it called on the city council "to restrain the running at large of cattle, horses, mules, swine, sheep, poultry, and geese."

The charter also provided for the more serious side of city building by establishing a board of health, authorizing the council to oversee road building and improvements, and regulating commerce. And, of course, the charter authorized the council to levy taxes.

Various amendments and additions were made to the charter through the years, with changes in the number of wards and number of councilmen elected. In 1909 a new concept of city government was recommended by a charter commission, which suggested that the affairs of the city could best be controlled and administered by a commission form of government. After more than a year of debate, the new charter was approved by the citizens in a special election in April 1911. It provided for a mayor and four councilmen.

The mayor headed the Department of Health, Sanitation, Police, and General Welfare. Control of four other city departments (Accounts and Finances; Parks, Public Grounds, Buildings and Fire Protection; Water Works and Sewers; and Streets and Alleys) was divvied up among the four councilmen.

The constitutionality of the commission charter was challenged in the courts, but the system was in full operation when the Minnesota Supreme Court upheld it on May 21, 1912. A.G. Meyer was the first mayor elected under the new system, and the first four councilmen were Robert Lamm, Ben Bangerter, Jr., J.D. Humiston, and Lawrence Henline. While there was an undercurrent of feeling that not every councilman was qualified to head the department assigned to him, the charter remained in effect, essentially unchanged, until it was replaced by a council-manager charter adopted in 1952.

Under this plan all discretionary powers, both legislative and executive, went to a city council elected by citizens at large and "subject to the initiative,

*The city charter, given to Mankato in spring 1868, led to the establishment of many councils, including one to oversee road building. This crew, depicted here in 1907 with pick and shovel, laid brick paving on North Front Street. The Hubbard Mill landmark chimney appears on the left next to the Stahl House. Courtesy, Blue Earth County Historical Society*

referendum, and recall powers of the people." The charter went on to give the council complete control over the city administration, but said it must "exercise this control exclusively through the city-manager." The city manager was the city's chief administrator, with vast powers to appoint or remove anyone from a department head to a secretary.

Some citizens openly opposed the city manager idea from its inception, but no concerted effort was made to abolish the system until a group that called itself Citizens for Good Government circulated a petition that forced an election on the issue in 1969. There were really two questions on that ballot: Should Mankato return to a ward system for the selection of city council members (for several years candidates from one area of the city had dominated the council and people in other areas bewailed their lack of representation), and should the council manager

form of government be replaced with a city administrator? Voters, by a good margin, approved the election of five council members by wards and one other by citizens at large. But the council-manager plan withstood the test when its opponents failed, by a narrow margin, to muster the required 55 percent of the vote.

In 1970, after the charter changes took effect, the office of mayor and all five council seats were filled in a regular election. Herbert Mocol, who had spearheaded Citizens for Good Government, was elected councilman at large. The author, who strongly supported the council-manager plan, was elected mayor by a comfortable margin. He was relected without opposition in 1972 and retired at the end of 1974. Mocol was elected to succeed him and served as mayor from 1975 through 1987.

Soon after the new council was installed in January 1971, a petition to discharge City Manager Bill Bassett, who had held the office for two years, was presented to the council and placed on file for consideration. It never surfaced again and Bassett still held the position two decades later.

A new charter commission was activated in 1985. After months of study the commission updated the charter but left the council manager plan intact. These revisions were adopted and became effective on November 9, 1987, by a unanimous vote of the city council.

Perhaps one of the prickliest political hot potatoes in Mankato history concerned efforts over the years to annex the city on the north bank of the bend of the river. Although the two towns never merged, North Mankato shared much of Mankato's history and development. After the Treaty of Traverse des Sioux opened a vast territory to settlement, numerous towns were platted by speculators but never developed. One was South Bend, just across the Blue Earth River from Mankato. Another was Kerns, a neighbor of North Mankato in the Belgrade Township area of Nicollet County. For years Kerns boasted a post office while North Mankato had none, but Kerns slowly died until only a creamery and a church were left. The church survived, but the creamery burned to the ground, leaving only a tall brick chimney that dominated the landscape until it too toppled. (North Mankato finally obtained its own post office in 1948.)

The river was a natural barrier to settlement in North Mankato, whose only access to Mankato was by two ferries, one near the present Sibley Park and the other at the river's bend where the first bridge was later built. North Mankato was laid out in 1857 by Isaac

Marks, Asa White, and Joseph Gunther, but a few years went by before development actually started.

In *The History of North Mankato,* published in 1977, it's reported that

*Gambling houses and brothels were scattered along the north side [of the river] close enough to the ferry landings to be convenient to patrons yet out of reach of the morals of local leaders.*

*One such ill-famed establishment, a gambler's hangout called O'Neill's, was where Jesse and Frank James, the Younger*

*In 1909 a new concept of city government suggested that the affairs of the city could best be administered by a commission form of government. The new commissioners worked out of the City Hall building located at Walnut and Front streets for many years. With some remodeling, the hall accomodated the police department, the city clerk's and engineer's offices, and the council chambers and courtroom. Courtesy, Blue Earth County Historical Society*

brothers, and a few other notorious outlaws rendezvoused on Sunday, September 3, 1876, before their famous bank robbery attempt at Northfield, Minnesota.

With the banishment of the Sioux Indians from Minnesota in 1863 and the end of the Civil War in 1865, the vast area acquired by treaty drew a flow of settlers through Mankato, and North Mankato also grew with the tide. The first railroad to Mankato in 1868 stimulated the economy of North Mankato as well, but the trans-river ferries proved inadequate for real growth. North Mankato's future depended on a bridge to cross the river, which at flood stage was too deep and turbulent for ferryboats and at low stage in summer months often was too shallow for the cumbersome flatboats.

That long-desired bridge became a reality in 1880. The Minnesota legisla-

ture had, in 1878, authorized the issuance of bonds to finance construction of a bridge. Blue Earth County, Mankato, Nicollet County, and Belgrade Township combined efforts to sell the bonds. Construction began in 1879 and the bridge was completed the next year, at a cost of $30,000. The iron structure was 810 feet long with three spans. One of those spans was mounted on a pivot to permit steamboats to pass through, even though the railroad had eliminated most river traffic by that time.

North Mankato boomed in the decade following the bridge opening. Industry came in 1886, when A.L. Wheeler and O.E. Bennett started a brick factory. Two other brickyards, the W.E. Stewart and the Shingles yards, soon followed. A few years later the North Mankato Brick Company also began operations. One by one, however, the brick makers closed their

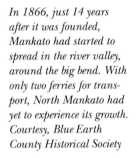

*In 1866, just 14 years after it was founded, Mankato had started to spread in the river valley, around the big bend. With only two ferries for transport, North Mankato had yet to experience its growth. Courtesy, Blue Earth County Historical Society*

plants, probably because they had exhausted the supply of readily available clay and because of competition from brickyards that made kiln-hardened products superior to their soft, common brick.

At this point North Mankato was still a part of Belgrade Township. But business leaders and citizens soon were engaged in spirited discussions over whether they should incorporate as a village or annex to Mankato. Independence would mean lower taxes, while annexation would provide better fire and police protection, schools, parks, postal services, and public utilities. Annexation would also mean easier access to the county seat at Mankato in Blue Earth County, as opposed to the Nicollet County seat at St. Peter, which was 12 miles distant.

In an election held on December 19, 1898, advocates of incorporation prevailed by a margin of 74 to 53. Nicollet County officials set December 31 as the date for a special election to permit the fledgling village to choose

its officials so that they could be on the job by early in the new year. Wendell Hodapp, a popular druggist, was elected the village council president. Other officials chosen were O.E. Bennett, Andrew W. Weimer, and Frank Wilds as trustees; Anders Anderson as recorder; W.E. Stewart as treasurer; S.A. Walrath and J.D. Tidland as justices of the peace; Smith Fuller and John Gyerik as constables; and Adolph Hintz as street commissioner.

The next hot topic in the new village concerned the sale of liquor. Evidently, the village council did not want to decide, because the choice of "license" or "no license" was placed on the ballot in the spring of 1900. Voters wasted no time in showing where they stood. By a 91-to-58 margin, they told the council "no license." North Mankato remained officially "dry" until the Prohibition Act was repealed in 1933.

As the incorporated village grew, civic improvements had top priority. A franchise was granted to the Mankato Gas and Electric Company to install gas mains, erect lines for electric service, and install streetlights. Another franchise was given to the Citizens and Northwest Telephone Company. A

*Growth of North Mankato spurted after the new iron bridge was completed in 1897 at the bend of the river. One span swung on a pivot to permit passage of steamboats. This photograph, taken from the North Mankato end of the bridge, shows the historic Saulpaugh Hotel and a grain storage elevator next to the levee. Courtesy, Blue Earth County Historical Society*

*North Mankato's first council president after it became a village in 1899 was Wendell Hodapp. Later Hodapp became chairman of the Nicollet County Board of Commissioners. Courtesy, City of North Mankato*

school district was created and the old schoolhouse enlarged, a village library was opened, a volunteer fire department was organized, and dikes were raised to protect the village from the frequent floodwaters of the Minnesota River.

But annexation to Mankato was an issue that kept coming back. Petitions were circulated in 1901 and 1905 asking for a special election to settle the issue once and for all. In 1905 somebody suggested changing the course of the river to make it flow closer to the edge of the bluff and thus around most of North Mankato. The key argument here was that because the river was the

*In 1907 the North Mankato city hall and public library occupied a small frame building next to the fire station on Belgrade Avenue. All were combined in a new municipal building in 1926. Courtesy, City of North Mankato*

boundary between Blue Earth and Nicollet counties, the plan would place North Mankato within the City of Mankato. This fantastic idea died quickly because of the enormity of the project and the prohibitive cost.

Still another annexation proposal surfaced in 1911, when both the North Mankato and Mankato commercial clubs unanimously endorsed the idea. This time, not surprisingly, the proposal died in the North Mankato Village Council. Another petition was floated in 1917 but it too was officially buried.

Construction of a new concrete bridge to replace the old iron structure

*The old Main Street Bridge built in 1917 carried foot and vehicle traffic between Mankato and North Mankato for 69 years and was probably the only bridge many Mankatoans ever knew. After the new Veterans Memorial Bridge was completed the old bridge was torn down and removed as the Corps of Engineers believed it would be a barrier to the free flow of the river between new flood walls and dikes. Courtesy, Blue Earth County Historical Society*

between the sister cities began in 1917. This proved to be another strong stimulus to North Mankato. The contract to build the bridge was awarded to the Gustav Widell Company of Mankato for $95,140. Designers looked ahead by including lampposts for streetlights and fixtures to carry cables for streetcars. Tracks were also laid in the roadbed, but the anticipated streetcar lines were never extended across the bridge to North Mankato. The concrete structure was widened and repaved in the 1970s to accommodate ever-increasing vehicular traffic. That project cost about $300,000, more than three times the bridge's original cost.

The venerable structure served well for 69 years before it was closed to traffic on May 15, 1986, and torn down. The U.S. Army Corps of Engineers said the bridge could be a barrier to free flowage because it stood below the concrete walls and dikes they had built to confine the river during floods. The magnificent new Veterans Memorial

Bridge, which met flood control requirements, replaced the old span. Contracts for the bridge totaled $12.2 million. With the added cost of highway changes and approaches, the final price tag was about $16 million.

Under state law, North Mankato had grown sufficiently by 1922 to become a city of the fourth class. In the first election under the new charter, voters wiped the slate clean and elected entirely new officials. D.O. Tenney was the first mayor; Victor Rydeen was voted recorder; R.W. Gosslee was treasurer; O. Rosler was justice of the peace; and F.L. Bennett, Sam Sandon, and John Koppen were aldermen. The mayor had the power to appoint an assessor, chief of police, engineer, and street commissioner.

Annexation champions still refused to give up the battle to become a part of a "greater" Mankato. In 1923, 508 of the city's 750 registered voters signed a petition to put annexation on the ballot during an election scheduled for June 18. Legal skirmishes followed. At issue was whether a public vote on annexation was permissible under state law. The go-ahead for the annexation vote finally arrived with a delegation from the state attorney general's office in St. Paul. But it was too late. Earlier the same evening the North Mankato City Council, assuming from an earlier interpretation that an annexation vote was illegal, canceled that part of the ballot. Despite public outcry, the council adamantly refused to reconsider its position no matter how many petitions might be presented. As *The History of North Mankato* put it, "What the council did, in essence, was to close the door on annexation, and, in the continuing history of North Mankato, it was a door that never again reopened."

As if to cement that declaration of independence, North Mankato built its own municipal building for $30,000 in 1926. City offices were located here, in addition to a public auditorium and rooms for police and fire equipment. More than 1,000 people attended dedication ceremonies on April 27. North

Mankato's growth slowed during the Depression and World War II but spurted again in the 1950s. A major building project in 1953 was the junior high school, which provided rooms and auxiliary areas for grades five through nine. That and the construction of Garfield Street cost $660,000.

The 1960s were an important decade for North Mankato. Recognizing that city business had become too extensive for part-time management, the council hired Bob Ringhofer as city superintendent in 1963. When North Mankato adopted a city administrator plan, the position was offered unanimously to Ringhofer. He still holds that office today.

Another major step was the decision to build a new municipal building at 1001 Belgrade Avenue. Outgoing mayor Howard Vetter presided over cornerstone laying ceremonies on December 28, 1967. The city council held its first meeting in its new chambers on December 9, 1969. The new municipal building housed the city staff, public library, and police and fire departments. Contracts for the building totaled $434,000, more than 14 times

*North Mankato was proud of its municipal building dedicated and completed in 1926 at a cost of $30,000. It housed city offices, the police department, a fire station, a library, and an all-purpose auditorium. Courtesy, City of North Mankato*

the cost of the 1926 structure.

The 1960s also saw the construction of Koppen Gardens, an eight-story, 76-unit apartment complex for senior citizens. North Mankato's park system was also greatly expanded and the city opened a swimming pool in Spring Lake Park. Looking to the future, the council ordained that real estate developers should pay a fee for each planned housing unit. The ordinance also gave the city first opportunity to buy land from developers for park purposes, thus avoiding the lengthy and costly process of condemnation.

Except for the matter of annexation, Mankato and North Mankato were good neighbors from their very beginnings. Today officials of the sister cities work together on transportation with the Mankato Area Transit System (MATS) serving both communities. The Blue Earth County Law Enforcement Center houses the county sheriff's department, the Mankato Police Department, and a county jail, and operates a joint dispatching office for the sheriff as well as Mankato and North Mankato police. The 911 emergency

call system includes North Mankato. In 1932, when North Mankato's water plant failed, the city was without water for a few hours until Mankato strung fire hoses across the Main Street Bridge.

By contract, North Mankato's waste water is pumped under the river to the Mankato treatment plant. Mankato's fire department will respond to a call for help from North Mankato. North Mankato's volunteers also respond if called to a major conflagration in Mankato. North Mankato also has representation on the Mankato Airport Advisory Committee.

North Mankato and Mankato consolidated their school districts in 1957 and their libraries are both part of the Minnesota Valley Regional Library. North Mankato also joins Mankato in the Minnesota Valley Council of Governments, organized in 1970 with Blue Earth, Nicollet, Brown, Waseca, and Le Sueur counties and the cities of Elysian, Janesville, Kasota, Le Sueur, New Ulm, St. Peter, and Waseca.

For a closer understanding of mutual problems and concerns, the councils of both

*Firemen manned the Central Fire Station on Second Street keeping teams of horses ready to respond to any alarm. Volunteers were also on call whenever needed. The city also housed one hose rig and a team of horses at fire stations on North Fourth Street and at the Y formed by South Front Street and Park Lane in West Mankato, where volunteer firemen met regularly and learned firefighting techniques. This image was made around 1910. Courtesy, Blue Earth County Historical Society*

cities attend joint meetings held at least every quarter. North Mankato participates in the Mankato Area Chamber of Commerce and the Greater Mankato Area United Way. It also holds its annual North Mankato Fun Days festival in conjunction with Mankato's Bend of the River celebration in July.

While North Mankato has only a few service stores and a small central business district (which includes the post office and the Valley National Bank), it has enjoyed tremendous growth and employment has risen substantially in the last 20 years. An industrial park of 300 acres with streets and utilities was created and has since been enlarged as plants have moved in and others expanded. Hundreds of acres of land in the hilltop area have been annexed and construction of homes has been sensational. Additional attractive land is available for further growth.

By the late 1980s North Mankato was no longer just a bedroom community of Mankato. Instead, it stood on its own, a well governed, thriving city of more than 10,000 happy and prosperous citizens.

## *A Tradition of Service*

### *Mankato Mayors*

| | | | | | |
|---|---|---|---|---|---|
| J.A. Wiswell | 1868-1870 | Chris Steiner | 1925-1927 | | |
| Z. Paddock | 1870-1872 | Frank J. Mahowald | 1927-1933 | | |
| J.J. Thompson | 1872-1875 | C.K. Mayer | 1933-1935 | | |
| J.A. Wiswell | 1875-1879 | Frank J. Mahowald | 1935-1937 | | |
| Edwin Bradley | 1879-1881 | Armin Kleinschmidt | 1937-1939 | | |
| J.A. Wiswell | 1881-1882 | Frank J. Mahowald | 1939-1941 | | |
| George Maxfield | 1882-1884 | C.K. Mayer | 1941-1947 | | |
| George M. Palmer | 1884-1886 | Rolande F. Johnson | 1947-1949 | | |
| George T. Barr | 1886-1887 | E.A. Hodapp | 1949-1951 | | |
| P.H. Carney | 1887-1888 | John Zotalis | 1951-1953 | | |
| A.R. Pfau | 1888-1891 | E.A. Hodapp | 1953-1956 | | |
| J.A. Willard | 1891-1893 | Rex Hill | 1956-1966 | | |
| Edgar Weaver | 1893-1897 | Clifford Adams | 1966-1971 | | |
| A.R. Pfau | 1897-1899 | Vernard E. Lundin | 1971-1975 | | |
| F.M. Currier | 1899-1901 | Herbert Mocol | 1975-1987 | | |
| Nic. Peterson | 1901-1903 | Vernon Carstensen | 1987- | | |
| Charles T. Taylor | 1903-1907 | | | | |
| J.W. Andrews | 1907-1909 | | | | |
| A.G. Meyer | 1909-1911 | | | | |
| Charles T. Taylor | 1911-1913 | | | | |
| A.G. Meyer | 1913-1916 | | | | |
| Robert Lamm | 1916-1917 | | | | |
| L.L. Champlin | 1917-1919 | | | | |
| Erastus V. Watters | 1919-1921 | | | | |
| W.A. Beach | 1921-1925 | | | | |

### *Mankato City Managers*

| | |
|---|---|
| Charles F. Trinkle | 1952-1954 |
| Harold B. Vasey | 1956-1960 |
| Erwin G. Hill | 1960-1966 |
| William A. Bassett | 1968- |

### *North Mankato Presidents*

| | |
|---|---|
| Wendell Hodapp | 1898-1902 |
| Nels Anderson | 1902-1904 |
| Q.M. Hagwall | 1904-1906 |
| J.B. Nelsen | 1906-1908 |
| Otto Neitge | 1908-1910 |
| J.B. Nelsen | 1910-1912 |
| W.H. Sharp | 1912-1914 |
| J.B. Nelsen | 1914-1918 |
| C.E. Ball | 1918-1922 |

### *North Mankato Mayors*

| | |
|---|---|
| D.O. Tenney | 1922-1924 |
| W.G. Fenger | 1924-1926 |
| Pat Kelly | 1926-1930 |
| Frank Neubert | 1930-1932 |
| D.E. Benson | 1933-1939 |
| Howard Wollam | 1940-1953 |
| Frank C. Daniels | 1954-1957 |
| Phil Lutzi | 1958-1959 |
| Henry Olson | 1960-1963 |
| Ray Eckes | 1965-1967 |
| Howard Vetter | 1968-1970 |
| Arnulf Ueland | 1970-1972 |
| David Carlson | 1973-1980 |
| David L. Dehen | 1981- |

*This 200 block on the west side of Front Street no longer exists. The Mankato State Bank closed in the early 1900s and Gene Coy's livery left the Front Street location years ago. Schmidt's Saddlery, the Wonderland Theater, a bicycle shop, and the L. Patterson Mercantile Company have all been relegated to history. Courtesy, Blue Earth County Historical Society*

# Mankato's Solid Foundation

The Mankato business community has always kept pace with changing times. In its pioneer days much activity developed around horsepower, with blacksmith shops, horseshoers, harness and saddle makers, and wagon and carriage manufacturers. Livery stables cared for horses by the day, week, or month, and some had carriages and horses for hire. By 1900 there were nine busy liveries.

One of these early enterprises that enjoyed extraordinary longevity was the Schmidt Saddlery Company. Founded in 1859 by Gottlieb Schmidt, this firm started out serving the leather needs of the horseman and farmer. Gradually, over four generations of family management, the merchandise shifted to cameras, photography supplies, luggage, purses, belts, and many other gift items until the firm was liquidated in 1986.

Mankato's oldest industry, the quarrying and fabrication of dolomitic limestone, was born only a year after the town was founded and survives to this day. When waters from Lake Agassiz poured out at the end of the Ice Age and formed the Minnesota River Valley, deep layers of limestone were left exposed in terraces between Mankato and Kasota. Unofficial records and memories indicate there were 28 quarries in the Mankato-Kasota area over the years, but many were small and provided stone only for the owner's use.

George Maxfield opened the first quarry at Mankato in 1853 and built his home, which still stands, with stone from that quarry. John R. Beatty, who became Maxfield's son-in-law, was a geologist who recognized the value of the limestone deposits and became a quarryman himself. He also developed processes to make lime and cement.

The heaviest need for limestone came when the railroads pushed westward and bought many tons of stone blocks for bridges. Some Mankato quarry operators became bridge builders themselves. Many public buildings in Mankato were built of limestone—the U.S. Post Office and the Blue Earth County Court House are prime examples—and foundations and trim for countless other structures came from local quarries, keeping the industry alive and prosperous.

Important names in the stone industry were Coughlan, Widell, Jefferson, Babcock and Wilcox, Breen, Bashaw, Fowler and Pay, and Vetter.

Only two companies exist today and both are nationally known. They are Mankato-Kasota Stone, Inc., operated by the fourth generation of Coughlans, and the Vetter Stone Company operated by four grandsons of Bernhard Vetter, a pioneer quarryman at Kasota. Both companies work several quarries that contain ledges of different colors. Stone from these two companies has been selected by many architects, including Cesar Pelli and Frank Lloyd Wright.

In the early days quarrymen produced lime by burning stone in huge kilns. Leading that segment of the industry were the Coughlans and Fowler and Pay. Beatty found a better alternative to slaked lime for mortar in masonry construction when he developed hydraulic cement made from limestone. In 1882 eastern capitalists came to Mankato and opened shop as the Standard Cement Company in West Mankato. But that plant was shut down the next year because of machinery failure.

Two of the partners in that venture, George H. Carney and Uriah Cummings, reopened the plant and formed the Mankato Cement Works. Carney bought out Cummings and in 1905 sold the business to his son, Harry E. Carney, who changed the name to the Carney Cement Company. In 1920 Carney developed a new product by blending lime and natural cement, which was given the name of Carney Bricklayer's Cement. But when a new product called Portland Cement came out, Carney's sales plunged, so he got

out of the cement business and dismantled the plant. The company then operated a rock wool insulation plant at the old Widell Klondike quarry. But that product, too, lost in competition with other types of insulation, and the name Carney became a part of Mankato history. Le Sueur Street, which ran past the original West Mankato plant, was renamed Carney Avenue.

Four generations of the Radichel family had more luck with the North Star Concrete Company, now a diversified firm with headquarters at Mankato. D.W. Radichel started making concrete drain tile in a small plant at Rapidan but moved in 1888 to a site on the Minnesota River in Mankato near Sibley Park. There he acquired 50 acres of railroad land, and he dredge mined sand from the riverbed for concrete mixing.

The company diversified and expanded as subsequent generations took over. When plastic became the industry standard for plumbing and other un-

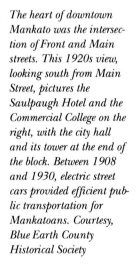

*The heart of downtown Mankato was the intersection of Front and Main streets. This 1920s view, looking south from Main Street, pictures the Saulpaugh Hotel and the Commercial College on the right, with the city hall and its tower at the end of the block. Between 1908 and 1930, electric street cars provided efficient public transportation for Mankatoans. Courtesy, Blue Earth County Historical Society*

dergrounds pipelines, concrete tile be- came obsolete. Not to be left behind, North Star set up a new plastic pipe di- vision with plants in three states.

North Star expanded concrete manufacturing beyond Mankato with its "queen" plant in Apple Valley, Minnesota, and others at Rochester, Minnesota, Sioux Falls, South Dakota, and Naperville, Illinois. In 1960 the company entered the prestressed con- crete construction industry with a plant in Osseo, Minnesota.

In Mankato in the 1980s, North Star also sold ready-mix concrete and sand and gravel mined at Judson and Kasota. The river no longer supplied the aggregate materials.

It is fortunate for historians that Mankato's progress was recorded in newspapers, starting only five years after Johnson and Jackson staked out the townsite. In 1989 only one newspaper, the *Free Press*, remained. Its roots went back to 1857, when Clinton Hensley and Frank Gunning hauled a printing press and other equipment from Kokomo, Indiana, and started the *Mankato Independent*, which was strongly and openly Republican. After Hensley died in 1863 his partner sold the *Independent* to Charles Slocum, who changed the name to the *Mankato Weekly Union*, prob- ably backing Abraham Lincoln and the Union cause in the Civil War.

Not to be outdone, John C. Wise,

*Mankato's oldest industry, the quarrying and fabrica- tion of dolomitic limestone, was created shortly after the town was founded. Courtesy, Blue Earth County Historical Society*

*Built in 1889 with Mankato limestone quarried specifically for the building, the Blue Earth County Court House stands today with no exterior changes, only interior remodeling. Courtesy, Blue Earth County Historical Society*

who had come from Superior, Wisconsin, started publishing the *Mankato Weekly Record,* to champion Democratic causes. Wise sold his *Weekly Record* in November 1868 to Orville Brown and J.T. Williams, who made a complete conversion from the Democratic to the Republican position. Wise jumped back into the fray and began publishing a new Democratic paper, the *Mankato Weekly Review.*

In 1879 James H. Baker bought both the *Union* and the *Record* and consolidated them into the *Mankato Weekly Free Press,* which started publication in January 1880. Baker sold the paper to L.P. Hunt in 1881, and on April 1, 1887, the weekly became the *Mankato Daily Free Press.* In 1892 the *Review* also appeared as a daily, but was bought out by the *Mankato Daily Free Press* in 1919. A new group of owners, including Charles Butler, M.D. Fritz, and I.N. Tompkins, ran the newspaper and a commercial printing plant for more than a decade.

In the aftermath of the 1929 stock market crash, a substantial block of *Free Press* stock was acquired from creditors by the First National Bank. James A. Callahan, who had been a publisher with the Hearst group in California and owner-publisher of a daily paper in St. Louis, agreed to buy the stock if enough additional shares could be accumulated to give him majority control. That arrangement was made and Callahan took over in the early 1930s.

When Callahan died of a heart attack on a train en route to a Florida vacation, his widow became the nominal publisher with editor Clifford H. Russell in charge of day-to-day operations. A few years later Jared How, a nephew of Mrs. Callahan, became the majority owner and publisher, and he and the newspaper gained wide acclaim and growth. In 1979 How retired and sold the paper to Ottaway Newspapers, Inc., a subsidiary of the Dow Jones Corporation, publishers of the *Wall Street Journal.*

*Depicted here in 1910 is the Mankato Post Office built in 1896. This public building was constructed with limestone quarried within the city. In 1932 an addition more than doubled its size and the clock tower was removed. Courtesy, Blue Earth County Historical Society*

The paper eventually dropped the descriptive "Daily" from its masthead and became simply the *Mankato Free Press*. As circulation increased to 17,500, in over 10 counties in south central Minnesota, it became a regional paper and became simply the *Free Press*.

Financial institutions also came to Mankato early on to keep pace with the town's rapid development. The oldest was the First National Bank, organized in 1868, and now called First Bank as part of the regional First Bank System. The National Citizens Bank, later the Northwestern National Bank and now simply Norwest Bank, was started in 1872. The Mankato Savings and Loan Association dates back to 1881, and years later became the First Federal Savings and Loan, finally becoming part of the Twin City Federal organization. The American Bank, organized in 1906 as the German American Bank, later

became the American State Bank. Today it is called simply the American Bank. The Security State Bank opened its doors in 1913, and the Bank of Commerce has been in business since 1934. Early in 1990 it became part of the MidAmerica system.

Other financial institutions that arrived over the years include the Valley National Bank, the Minnesota Valley Savings Bank, the First State Bank, the Wells Federal Savings and Loan, the Metropolitan Federal Bank, Farm Credit Services, Minnesota Valley Federal Credit Union, and the State Capitol Credit Union at Mankato State University.

Much of the prosperity enjoyed in the maturing town came thanks to the area's rich environment, the land supporting a variety of industries that were rooted in the soil. A large-scale flour-milling operation arrived in 1878 when

R.D. Hubbard, George M. Palmer, and William Pearson founded the Hubbard Milling Company. Palmer succeeded Hubbard as president in 1906, and under his leadership the company supplemented flour milling by pioneering a concentrate for feeding poultry and livestock. Palmer and the Hubbard Milling Company never looked back. By the late 1980s Hubbard had operations in a dozen different states, and its pet food, molasses concentrates, feed supplements, and turkey products were being shipped all over the world. The company's birthplace, the flour mill at Mankato, was sold to Cargill in 1984.

There have been several large lumber yards and millwork operations in Mankato and North Mankato over the years. Many Mankatoans remember the Knoff Millworks and Hager Manufacturing Company. But only two complete lumber and wood finishing operations still existed in the late 1980s. The Neubert Millwork Company and the Lindsay Sash and Door Company both occupy large new plants in North Mankato.

Dairy operations also made their mark in Mankato. The Creamery Package Company, which oldtimers called "the tub factory," was at its peak in 1885. But a wider swath in dairying was cut by J.C. Marlow, who came to Mankato from Wisconsin in 1914. Marlow brought with him a mild-action

*One of the oldest banks in Mankato, still strong and now in new quarters, is the First Bank, formerly the First National Bank founded in 1868. The original building is shown here. Courtesy, Blue Earth County Historical Society*

milking machine he had developed to reduce the incidence of mastitis in dairy cattle. He was also a breeder of purebred Holstein cattle, and animals from his Mankato Holstein farm won state and national grand championships. Calves from Marlow's Ormsby strain helped to improve the production and profitability of many herds. Marlow's barn, a showplace, is listed on the National Register of Historic Sites. The Marlow milker gave way to the new pipeline milking system and was discontinued in 1970, but the new owners retained the Marlow name as distributor for the Conde Company and other dairy farm equipment.

When a small group of Mankato investors sensed that soybeans were becoming a major crop on southern Minnesota farms, they gutted their Minnesota Pipe and Tile Company building on the banks of the Blue Earth River and installed a single-expeller soybean processing plant. They sold the business at the start of World War II to a Washington State farm feed cooperative

that shipped its entire soybean-meal production to the West Coast.

After the war the plant was sold to the Andreas family of Iowa, and when Lowell Andreas came to Mankato to manage the operation, he brought the Honeymead name with him. The plant was enlarged, the solvent process of oil extraction was installed, and bean storage facilities were built.

In 1962 the operation was sold to the Farmers Union Grain Terminal Association which (with the help of tax increment financing from the city) doubled the size of the plant at a cost of several million dollars. Capacity of the plant reached a maximum of 80,000 bushels of soybeans a day.

Another homegrown company in the agricultural field was the Ramy Seed Company founded by Roy Ramy in 1932. More than half a century later, Ramy was still busy processing alfafa and clover seed, hybrid corn, grasses, turf products, and birdseed in plants at Mankato, LaCrosse, Wisconsin, and Wright City, Missouri. Much of what

*The First Bank's drive-in at Hickory and Second streets was originally the site of the Mankato Fruit Company, seen here. To the left is a printing office and a monument company with its samples displayed on the sidewalk. Courtesy, Blue Earth County Historical Society*

Ramy sold is grown on company-owned farms. The company markets its farm and garden seeds in seven Midwestern states and exports some products to Canada, Europe, and the Far East.

Public utilities, which transformed both industry and everyday life in Mankato and North Mankato, also had their beginnings in locally owned enterprises. In 1883 the Mankato Gas Light Company was formed by O.C. McCurdy, L. Patterson, and S.W. Kanke. The company produced gas by imperfect combustion of bituminous coal, which was pressurized by a huge piston and forced into underground mains along Front Street, at first serving 115 business places and lighting 33 street lamps. Later, the gas mains were extended to most of the city. Coke, a by-product of gas production, was sold for heating fuel.

J.L. Watters and C.M. Marsh started the Mankato Electric Light Company in 1885, and in 1896 the two

utilities merged to become the Mankato Gas and Electric Light Company. This business was acquired by the Byllesby Company in 1910 and became the Consumers Power Company. This company built a hydroelectric plant on the Blue Earth River near Rapidan, which began generating power on March 11, 1911. Five years later Consumers became a part of the Northern States Power Company. The dam across the Blue Earth was heavily damaged by the 1965 flood and was abandoned. Northern States turned the property over to Blue Earth County, which constructed a new bridge to replace the narrow roadway on the dam. The generating plant was restored by private capital but has not been effective or profitable because of the low water level in dry seasons. With the arrival of piped-in natural gas, Northern States sold its gas interests to the Minnesota Valley Natural Gas Company, which today is part of the Minnegasco system.

*LEFT: The Citizens National Bank and the Star Clothing House were among Front Street establishments that flourished for a time but then sold their assets or closed their doors in the early 1900s. Courtesy, Blue Earth County Historical Society*

*BELOW: Mankato Mills was a sucessful company and major Mankato business in the early 1890s. About 150 employees manufactured 1,200 dozen pairs of Armor Clad stockings each day. Courtesy, Blue Earth County Historical Society*

Telephone service began in 1898 when a group of businessmen formed the Mankato Citizens Telephone Company. Incorporators of the company were Lorin Cray, Henry E. Hance, William A. Funk, J.H. Jones, Ed Staede, F. Kron, W.N. Plymat, H.A. Patterson, John C. Wise, Jr., A.G. Bierbauer, Nic. Peterson, John Klein, John B. Meagher, and O.W. Schmidt. The man who was to become president and general manager for many years, Peter M. Ferguson, joined the company as wire chief in 1907.

In April 1969 the company formed Mid-Communications, Inc., and acquired the small telephone exchanges in Blue Earth County, giving private-line dial service to more than 7,700 subscribers on farms and in the towns of Cambria, Lake Crystal, Garden City, Vernon Center, Amboy, Mapleton,

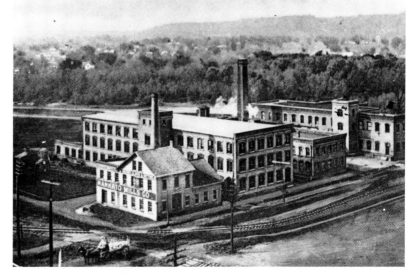

Pemberton, Good Thunder, St. Clair, Eagle Lake, and Madison Lake. In the late 1980s there were more than 25,000 subscribers in the Mankato-North Mankato area and Mid Communications was one of the few independent telephone companies left in Minnesota.

*The Hubbard House, built in 1871 by R. D. Hubbard and extensively remodeled in 1888, has recently been restored and furnished to its original grandeur by the Blue Earth County Historical Society. Hubbard was the major cofounder of Hubbard Milling Company and its president from 1878 until his death in 1905. Courtesy, Blue Earth County Historical Society*

The power of the new technology sparked new types of industry in Mankato. J. Fred Krost was a clerk in the Fisher Clothing store, when he figured out a way to branch out on his own. One of his duties was to turn off the display window lights at 10 o'clock each evening. In his nightly walks between home and store he reasoned that some mechanical device could be made to turn off the lights at any preset time. He experimented with switches hooked into an alarm clock and it worked. That put an end to his night walks in rain, sleet, snow, or cold.

Krost then started the Automatic Electric Company to make his time-automated switches. The business struggled for several years before the bugs were worked out. During World War II Automatic Electric had contracts with Collins Radio of Cedar Rapids, Iowa, and made components for that firm. Krost sold his business, which had employed many Mankato workers, to the Telex Corporation. Telex built a substantial plant in North Mankato, but was taken over by the Midtex Corporation, which closed the plant and moved to Texas.

Another Mankato company that took advantage of advancing technology dated back to 1876 when Lorenz Mayer, an immigrant from Germany, started a blacksmith and machine shop on North Front Street. Three sons, Louis, Lorenz, and Conrad, learned the trade from their father and opened a new shop on West Vine Street in 1891. Conrad left to start his own shop.

In 1894 Louis, an acknowledged mechanical genius, invented a trip hammer called the Little Giant. It proved to be the company's major product for years. Fire destroyed the Mayer Brothers foundry in 1901, but the firm immediately hired J.B. Nelsen to build a two-story factory on an adjoining site. With Louis as inventor and designer, Mayer Brothers began manufacturing

*The Palmer Centennial Place, featuring the restored carriage house for the Hubbard mansion, was the gift of Hubbard Milling Company to honor George M. Palmer, a co-founder and company president of Hubbard Milling from 1906 to 1939. The carriage house, seen here, was moved brick by brick from its original location to the new site, which adjoins the mansion grounds and is surrounded by Victorian gardens. Courtesy, Blue Earth County Historical Society*

boilers, gas and steam engines, hoists, steel beams, clothes reels, ditching machines, lathes, band saws, circle saws, drill presses, road graders, and Little Giant tractors.

In 1904 the company built a few four-wheel-drive trucks for Rosenberger and Currier, one of which was sold to Hubbard Milling Company to replace horse-drawn wagons for deliveries. Louis designed and built a V-8 engine when they were still in the experimental stage in the automobile industry. He mounted the engine in his own chassis with wooden spokes and solid rubber tires. A custom-made wooden body had seating space for seven passengers. The car was so big that greatly impressed Mankatoans called it the "Titanic."

Because of a lack of financing and marketing skills, the company went out of business for a time but reincorporated in 1909. Three years later the Little Giant farm tractor was enjoying good sales but once again heavy bor-

rowing brought financial difficulty. The company was taken over by the First National Bank, with O.M. Thatcher as manager. The Mayer Brothers name was dropped in favor of Little Giant.

Thatcher left the company in 1923 and directors elected L.J. Fazendin to succeed him. In 1943 Fazendin's son-in-law, G.A. "Jerry" Dotson eventually took over as general manager and the company took on his name. The Little Giant trip hammer was in demand in machine shops during World War II and government contracts often specified "Little Giant or equal." The Company also manufactured lids for armored tanks, drums for steel cables on navy vessels, and nose cones for bombers. In the postwar period the Dotson Company's emphasis turned to foundry work, and the firm developed a nationwide business based on its ability to produce quality castings in many metals.

Even before Pearl Harbor plunged the United States into World War II, a

*ABOVE: Log ties lying on the ground in the 400 block of South Front Street provided the bed for streetcar tracks. Mankato's first public transportation began operations in 1886 and was provided by streetcars pulled along the tracks by horses. Courtesy, Blue Earth County Historical Society*

*RIGHT: The Mankato Street Railway System gave passenger service to a limited area of town. The horse-drawn cars ran from 1886 to 1895, when the system proved unprofitable and the lines stopped running. Courtesy, Blue Earth County Historical Society*

small company in Mankato, called Mico, was manufacturing parts needed for military equipment. Mico's main product was its patented two-stage power brake cylinder that has been the heart of the business ever since. After the war Mico consolidated with Minnesota Automotive and in 1982 built a new plant in North Mankato. That plant employs 300 people. Branch plants were located in Los Angeles, Great Britain, and Australia. By 1989 Mico was designing and manufacturing hydraulic brake systems for automobiles and trucks and self-propelled industrial equipment for Clark Equipment company, Bendix, John Deere, Allis Chalmers, General Dynamics, FMC Corporation, and Caterpillar Tractor Company.

Another Mankato firm that contributed to the war effort was the Kato Engineering Company. Kato had been established by L.A. Wilkinson and E.J. Jenson well before the outbreak of World War II. After they abandoned their efforts, the new owner, Cecil H. Jones, switched from sales to manufacturing products of his own—chiefly the portable generator that brought the company into national prominence. When the war came, Kato was swamped with orders for electrical generators for naval vessels, field hospitals, army field headquarters, the Signal Corps, the Sea Bees, and other. Following the war Kato's prominence in its field continued to grow. Jones died in 1976, and his estate sold the company to the Reliance Electric Company of Chicago. Since then Kato has opened a large new plant in North Mankato, where more than 500 employees make generators of all sizes

*The advent of electricity introduced a new era of public transportation with the electric streetcar. In 1908 the Mankato Electric Traction Company ran its first cars. The main line ran from May Street on North Broad to Vine, along Vine to Front Street and through the downtown business district to Sibley Park. Depicted here after a heavy snowfall in 1908 are streetcars on Front Street. The Mankato Electric Traction Company cleared its tracks through town with plows and sweepers before any other vehicles could move. Double tracks made it possible for cars to meet on their runs to either end of the city. Courtesy, Blue Earth County Historical Society*

*Local women operated the switchboards for the Mankato Citizens Telephone Company, which was formed by a group of businessmen in 1898 to provide telephone service to residents. Courtesy, Blue Earth County Historical Society*

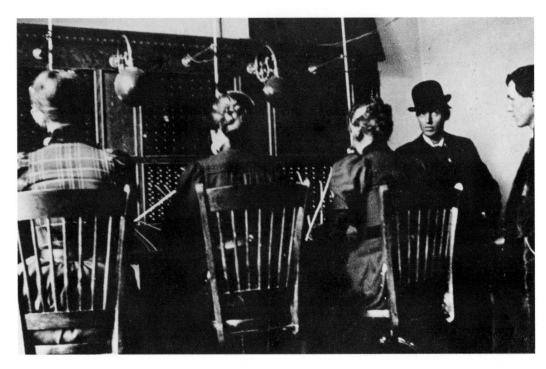

for national and international markets.

The economic upheaval after the war brought on another generation of Mankato industries—the packaging and distribution of the proliferating array of consumer goods. The Mankato Corporation had actually been around since 1905, when it started making cardboard cartons and gift boxes. E.W. Foster became the sole owner in 1914 and continued the business as the Mankato Paper Box Company. Eventually, the business expanded to include the production of plastic containers, custom-formed displays, and custom packaging. The business was sold to the Bemis Corporation in 1968, and two decades later it employed 125 people. Custom plastic-thermal forming accounted for 75 percent of its volume, although folding cardboard cartons were still in the product line.

Another packaging firm, National Poly Products, Inc., made plastic film for food processors and manufacturers. It was organized in 1959 by three

Mankato men, Fred Buscher, Sumner Carlstrom, and Frank Hecht. When temporary quarters in the last of the Bierbauer Brewery buildings proved too small, the company built a new plant on Third Avenue in 1970. The company became part of the Atlantic Group, which is listed on the American Stock Exchange.

The City of Mankato did its share to attract new industries. The city acquired the grounds occupied by the Mankato Fair just after the turn of the century. A large part of the property was sold off to the Continental Can Company in 1942.

Continental constructed a plant to manufacture metal cans principally for the Green Giant Company then headquartered in Le Sueur. Production of cans for peas and sweet corn hit a peak in 1970 when more than 500 workers were required to keep the cans rolling 24 hours a day. Business fell off when Green Giant began making its own containers and when other canners showed a preference for welded cans rather than the soldered type made by Continental.

Beverage cans replaced vegetable cans but that line also was discontinued in 1978. The fate of the plant was in jeopardy until it was sold to a private company, Peter Kiewit and Sons of Omaha, in 1984. The plant was remodeled and equipment installed to make flip-top can ends for the beer and soft drink industries. At last word, business remained brisk with customers from many states, including Wis-Pak in North Mankato, Coke Midwest in Minneapolis, and the Heileman brewery in La Crosse, Wisconsin.

The competition was keen when Cotter and Company, headquartered in Chicago, decided to locate a regional distribution center in Minnesota or Wisconsin, but Mankato was up to the task. The complete cooperation of the city council, the Chamber of Commerce, the Mankato Industrial Corporation, and several key citizens resulted in the selection of Mankato for the center. The city purchased land in the north end of the city in an industrial area with highway railroad, water, sewer, and electric power all available. Groundbreaking ceremonies were held in 1974, with Rudy Perpich, then Minnesota's lieutenant governor (later governor) taking part.

Cotter completed the 320,000-square-foot computerized warehouse and it was stocked and ready to make shipments on January 1, 1977. The Mankato facility was one of 15 warehouses at strategic points throughout the United States serving more than 5,000 customers. The Mankato warehouse, with 108 employees, supplied 329 True Value stores and 176 V&S variety stores in Minnesota, Iowa, North

*Jacob B. Nelsen, born in Denmark in 1863, came to North Mankato in 1887. He became a contractor and built many public buildings in North Mankato and Mankato. He also served as president of the village council for eight terms. Courtesy, City of North Mankato*

Dakota, South Dakota, Wisconsin, upper Michigan, and part of Nebraska.

One of the newest and most successful industries in the Mankato area was started in 1964 by W.A. "Al" Sween. Working in the basement of his home, his first product was a nonaerosol deodorant called Hex-On and was soon followed by Sween Cream, a hand and body lotion. Two friends who were pharmaceutical salesmen sold the products to hospitals and nursing homes along with their regular lines.

When assistants couldn't produce enough of the two products Sween organized the Sween Corporation in

1973. After operating out of several temporary locations in Rapidan, Lake Crystal, and Mankato, Sween completed a 100,000-square-foot building with offices, laboratories, and production facilities in the North Mankato industrial park. He held an open house in September 1989.

Sween has since expanded its product line to include a long list of lotions, ointments, sprays, powders, and cleaning compounds for personal care. Those products were sold in all 50 states and parts of Canada by a direct sales force of 50. The North Mankato plant employed 125 men and women.

The largest corporation by far in the Mankato-North Mankato area also started as a basement industry. The Taylor Corporation originated in 1945 when William Carlson opened the Carlson Letter Service in the basement of his home. Business outgrew the basement shop and Carlson moved to a

larger building on South Front Street later occupied by the Salvation Army. Here he branched into a more specialized business, printing wedding invitations and stationery.

Glen Taylor, a farm boy from Comfrey, Minnesota, came to Mankato in 1959 to attend Mankato State College. He secured a job with the Carlson Wedding Service to finance his education and finished a four-year course in three years. Carlson told Taylor he would match any teaching position salary that Taylor might be offered. He cast his lot with Carlson.

Soon after Taylor joined the company, Carlson built a new plant in North Mankato and adopted the new name of Carlson Craft. That plant was expanded three times in the next 12 years. In 1967 Carlson sold stock to Taylor and two other key employees, Jim Holland and Merlyn Anderson. When Carlson retired on January 1, 1975, he sold his majority

*One of the very few four-wheel-drive trucks manufactured in Mankato for Rosenberger and Currier was purchased by Hubbard Milling Company, replacing horse power for city deliveries. Jake Wellington took over the steering wheel instead of reins as Archie McCloud observed from the mill door. Courtesy, Hubbard Milling Company*

interest to Taylor.

Taylor created the Taylor Corporation as a holding company and since 1974 growth has been meteoric. In the late 1980s Carlson Craft plants produce more than half of all wedding invitations sold in the United States.

The company was housed in the North Mankato industrial park, where its five plants occupied more than 600,000 square feet. Taylor employed 2,500 people in 11 states. It also held banks in North Mankato, Fairfax, and Hector, Minnesota, although printing still accounted for about 80 percent of the corporation's revenues. The 1987 acquisition of C & H Printing, Inc., of Peoria gave Taylor its fourth printing company in Illinois. The North Mankato complex

also included a $400,000 day-care center for employees' preschool children, subsidized in large part by Taylor. For building one of Minnesota's 20 largest private businesses, *Corporate Report*, a Minneapolis publication, named Taylor Minnesota's Executive of the Year in 1986.

A national and international company, Johnson Fishing, Inc., was born in Mankato when fishing pals Lloyd Johnson and Warren Denison teamed up to develop and market the Johnson free-spinning reel, which eliminated backlash in bait casting. Johnson reels, other fishing tackle, and an electric trolling motor named MinKota were popular across America and in several foreign countries.

*This 20-foot metal lathe, new in 1915, went to war in 1917, turning out parts and repairs for armament plants vital to winning World War I. This lathe is still a basic part of the Enterprise Machine shop today. Originally, it was belt driven from a central power shaft but today it has its own electric motor. Courtesy, Enterprise Machinery*

*J. M. Halfhill, a prominent businessman around 1900, created attention when he sallied forth in this rig, called a skeleton wagon, drawn by a pair of magnificent Arabian horses. The photo probably was taken by George Keene, whose studio is shown behind the horses. Halfhill was founding partner of the L. Patterson Mercantile Company. Courtesy, Blue Earth County Historical Society*

Two brothers, Robert "Bob" Frederick and Marcel "Sal" Frederick, were small restaurant operators in 1963 when they secured a Small Business Administration loan to build their first Happy Chef restaurant on Highway 169. That restaurant proved to be the first of 56 Happy Chef restaurants in seven Midwestern states. Today the second generation, Tom and Bill Frederick, directs the still-growing chain.

No history of Mankato industry would be complete without including

the Truth Tool Company, launched in the early 1920s by Arthur E. Cowden, a blacksmith by trade who developed a method of hardening steel. Truth Tool was a major Mankato company until Cowden's death, when it was sold to the Owatonna Tool Company, which relocated the firm to complement its own tool manufacturing business.

Other new industries sprang up in the electronic and computer age, and by 1989 the Mankato phone directory listed 70 manufacturers, employing a

fourth of the area's total work force. Fifteen of those manufacturers were selling their products internationally.

A sizable number of Mankato business people also put their energy into providing amenities on the home front. Anthony J. Busch, an immigrant from Germany, came to Mankato in 1875, erected the Busch Building at the corner of Mulberry and North Front streets, and opened a retail grocery. An even larger firm establishing Mankato as a wholesale grocery supply center was the L. Patterson Mercantile Company. Founded in 1884 by L. Patterson, J.M. Halfhill, and A. Zimmerman, the firm continued a widespread business (with branches in the Dakotas) until it closed in 1956. In the decades that fol-

lowed the number of these neighborhood groceries went as high as 56, but the advent of chain stores and supermarkets doomed many of them. The Busch operation survived by going into the wholesale grocery business. But by the late 1980s the Mankato yellow pages listed only 6 supermarkets and 11 quick-stop mini-markets.

Mankatoans could dash over to the local department store as early as 1858. That's the year George E. Brett founded Brett's department store. Five generations later Brett's was still going strong, with stores in Mankato, Owatonna, Faribault, Hutchinson, Fairmont, and New Ulm.

Before women's stores became popular, city directories listed as many

*Before the days of chain supermarkets, the L. Patterson Mercantile Company distributed grocery supplies from their South Front Street building. Depicted here are the sharply dressed office managers and employees who ran the business. Courtesy, Blue Earth County Historical Society*

as 48 dressmakers, but not one has survived. There were once just as many millinery shops, but when hats no longer appeared in the Easter parade, they too closed their doors.

In the heart of downtown Mankato three specialty stores—F.W. Woolworth, S.S. Kresge, and H.L. Green—stood side by side in the busiest block of early South Front Street. Among the furniture stores that once served the community, only Landkamer's still carried on in the same old stand, even surviving a disastrous fire in the 1930s.

Before appliance stores sold electric refrigerators to most households, four companies delivered ice on regularly established routes. In the early days ice was harvested from the Minnesota River in the dead of winter and packed in sawdust in sheds called icehouses. The sawdust was the insulation that kept the

ice cakes from thawing in the warm days of summer until they were uncovered and loaded for delivery.

Through the bitter depression years of the 1930s there were only a few restaurants in Mankato and North Mankato. In 1989 there were 66, many of them fast-food drive-ins and pizza shops. Prior to the implementation of the Prohibition Amendment in 1920, Mankato had 35 saloons. After repeal of the 18th Amendment in 1933, Mankato qualified under state regulations for 13 liquor licenses, plus off-sale shops and many taverns with beer licenses.

Mankato joined the world of radio when station KYSM was incorporated by the F.B. Clements Company, going on the air on July 12, 1938. Its transmission tower was erected on the hill in North Mankato with its studios in Mankato. Later the offices and studios moved to

a new building on grounds adjacent to the tower.

The Minnesota Valley Broadcasting Company, headquartered at Willmar, went on the air with station KEYC on April 9, 1950, and added KDOG, an FM rock station, on April 1, 1985. Latecomers in radio broadcasting were KEEZ, KSMU-FM at Mankato State University, the local studios for KXLP-KNUJ of New Ulm, and KGAC, a public radio station with studios at Gustavus Adolphus College in St. Peter.

KEYC, with studios in North Mankato, made television reception available to a wide area of Southern Minnesota on November 29, 1960. Some two decades later the television options had exploded, with Cablevision of Mankato offering color transmission on 32 channels, including one dedicated to public access.

Mankato was somewhat somnolent prior to World War II, but came to life quickly when the war was over. The shopping area had been concentrated in downtown Mankato but soon started

moving to the hilltop on Madison Avenue, where development was rapid. For many years the only business on the hilltop avenue was the Windmiller's greenhouses and floral shop. The first businesses to follow Windmiller's were the Hilltop Tavern, still noted for its hamburgers; Salfer's Grove, a drive-in for root beer, malts, and food; a small "ma and pa" cabin-type motel, and Jovaag's root beer stand.

The first substantial building on Madison Avenue was Lewis Eastgate (housing a drug and variety store and a food market), and it was soon followed by the Belle Mar Mall. The Madison Avenue strip boomed after completion of the Madison Avenue Shopping Center in 1968. Its anchors were Sears and Woolworth's stores, with spaces for 55 smaller shops.

Businesses of every description followed—office buildings, medical clinics, super food markets, automobile dealers, service stations, banks, chain stores, variety chain stores, numerous fast-food restaurants, Menard's huge

*FACING and LEFT: Three department stores dominated Mankato's downtown for many years. At Front and Jackson streets was J.B. and D. Richards, (facing page). After a fire it was rebuilt as a four-story building, and was later the location of the S & L store. The building, which included the popular Richards Hall, still stands today and is attached to the Mankato Mall. The George E. Brett building at Jackson and Front streets,(left) is still the flagship and home office for the Brett's department store chain, which was founded in 1858. The Leader (not shown) at Main and Front streets became Salet's and remained in business until the 1970s, when it was removed for urban renewal. Courtesy, Blue Earth County Historical Society*

*This contemporary interior scene of the Mankato Mall was once the 300 block of South Front Street. Stores and shops on both sides of the covered mall were renovated when they fronted the mall rather than the street. Courtesy, Blue Earth County Historical Society*

lumber yard and building supply store—and eventually lined the rebuilt Madison Avenue for more than a mile. Professional offices, condominiums, and apartments sprang up on adjacent streets. Two more shopping malls, which would be Mankato's largest, were in the planning stages.

Meanwhile, urban renewal became a priority as a result of the Active Community Thought program. The belief that retail business belonged in a central downtown area was threatened by the Madison Avenue development. A lack of parking space in central downtown prompted the city council to create a parking district with an advisory group to study possible ways to relieve that problem. Several off-street parking lots were created, and a multilevel ramp with

352 stalls was completed in 1967 in time for the Christmas shopping season.

Shoppers resented paying parking fees downtown knowing there was ample parking around the Madison East Mall, and they preferred shopping under one roof in inclement weather. After long and difficult discussions, the decision was reached to build a downtown mall. But tearing down a block or more of buildings was considered unreasonable and prohibitively expensive.

Ultimately, the city decided to close off two blocks of Front Street in the heart of the shopping district, construct a roof over the vacated street, develop that space into attractive courts and a few kiosks, and tie the existing buildings into the overall structure.

Owners modernized their buildings with new fronts and new display windows, and installed sprinkler systems for fire protection.

The mall proved successful but the parking problems persisted. Another ramp with 449 stalls was built in 1970 at the foot of Walnut Street near the mall, with connection to 113 more spaces in the lower level of the new Holiday Inn, which was erected on the site of the historic Saulpaugh Hotel. Finally, another ramp with 736 spaces was built on Pike Street behind the mall, making a total of 1,690 spaces plus metered open lots and meters along the parking district streets.

In 1990 civic and business leaders were still studying ways to expand the downtown mall, attract new businesses and offices, and build a civic center near the mall. Objections that arose from cutting off through traffic on Front Street, perhaps forever, were mitigated by completion of Riverfront Drive skirting the mall area and connecting to the north and south ends of the city.

## Long-Lived Businesses

A list of long-lived businesses was complied in 1988 by the City of Mankato in observance of the 120th anniversary of its charter. Firms that served the Mankato-North Mankato region for more than 100 years included:

Brett's Department Store (1858)
First Bank (1868)
Martin and Hoerr Jewelers (1870)
Norwest Bank (1872)
First Federal Savings and Loan (1881)
Theodore Williams Insurance Company (1883)
August Deike Transfer, Inc. (1886)
Hilltop Florists (1886)
Cheever and Asleson Architecture (1878)

Those on the 75-year list include the following:

Ben Deike Transfer and Storge (1891)
Hick's Studio (1894)

Piper, Jaffray and Hopwood (1895)
Kersten's Furs (1897)
Landkamer's Furniture (1898)
Blethen, Gage and Krause (1900)
Cuddy Mechanical Contractors (1900)
Farrish, Johnson and Maschka (attorneys) (1901)
Willard Agency (real estate and insurance) (1901)
Goodman Jewelers (1907)
J. C. Marlow Milking Machine Company (1908)
B. H. Chesley (automobiles and trucks) (1910)
Clements Chevrolet (1913)
Mocol's Super Market (1914)
Southern Minnesota Construction Company (1914)
Schwickert's (1906)

The city also awarded certificates to 50-year-old firms:

Hagen Hardware (1916)
J.C. Penney (1917)
Snilsberg Danish Insurance (1918)

Artcraft Photo Service (1919)
Mankato Oil Company (1919)
Stan A. Smith Jewelers (1919)
National Bushing and Parts Company (1920)
Demaray Electric (1922)
Matt J. Graif Clothing (1924)
Prudential Insurance (1924)
Brett's Beauty Salon (1928)
C and N Sales (1928)
Cloverdale of Minnesota, Inc. (1928)
Meyer and Sons (1931)
Southern Valley Co-op (1931)
Lundberg Furs and Clothing (1931)
Kagermeier, Skaar and Paulsen (1932)
Ramy Seed Company (1932)
Atwood Realty (1934)
M and M Signs (1935)
Jakobs Lumber (1935)
Michels Motors (1936)
Investors Diversified Services (1936)
Artcraft Press (1938)
Key City Oil Company (1938)
Paper Service Company (1938)

*Education was of primary importance to Mankato's early settlers. West Mankato's growth required another elementary school and this structure was built in 1885. It was replaced by what is now the Roosevelt School. Courtesy, Blue Earth County Historical Society*

# *The Good Life*

**W**hen hardy pioneers—many of them immigrants from northern Europe—came to the frontier village of Mankato, they brought their religion and their culture with them. Their first thoughts after they built shelters for their families were places to worship and schools for their children.

Methodists organized the first congregation when the Mankato settlement was barely a year old. At first members met regularly for worship in whatever room or hall was available, until their first church was built in 1866.

German Catholics began arriving in 1854 and promptly built their first building. But it was not until 1873 that they dedicated their beautiful church, known as the Church of St. Peter and Paul.

The first Presbyterian Church was founded in 1855, and its members built a handsome stone edifice at Broad and Hickory. Two years later the women of the congregation raised $300 to buy a bell for the church steeple. For many years it served as the town bell, sounding alarms as well as joyous occasions, like the signing of the Armistice on November 11, 1918. With some additions and alterations, this venerable church still houses an active congregation.

The Baptists organized in 1859 and erected their house of worship on Broad Street in 1868. Immanuel Lutheran Church was formed by a group of Germans in 1866. The oldest of three small Norwegian Lutheran congregations was established in 1867.

These three churches merged to form Bethlehem Lutheran Church in 1919. Many of the early churches started by northern Europeans—Germans, Norwegians, and Swedes—worshipped at first in their native tongues.

Other Mankato churches that served the community for more than 100 years were: St. John's Episcopal (1866), First Christian (1868), Hilltop Methodist (1870), First Congregational (1870), Seventh Day Adventist (1874), St. John's Catholic (1884), and Grace Lutheran (1887).

By 1989 there were more than 43 denominations represented in Mankato and North Mankato. Over the years ecumenical dialogues and joint services were common. In 1976 three Mankato congregations—Centenary Methodist, First Baptist, and First Congregational—joined hands and built the Multi-Church Center on the site of the original Methodist church. Each congregation could hold services in either of two sanctuaries, and all shared the operation and maintenance costs. This unique arrangement attracted national attention.

Mankato's first school was in session by 1853 when two pioneer women, Sarah Jane Hanna and Mary Ann Thompson, started private classes for children. In 1855 a public school was organized and citizens elected three trustees. Land for the school was given by John S. Hinckley and a fund was subscribed for the building. When the one-

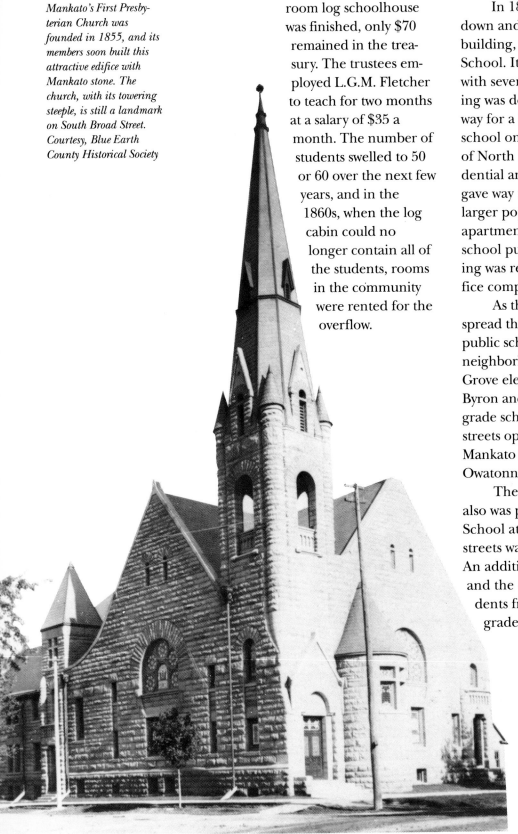

*Mankato's First Presbyterian Church was founded in 1855, and its members soon built this attractive edifice with Mankato stone. The church, with its towering steeple, is still a landmark on South Broad Street. Courtesy, Blue Earth County Historical Society*

room log schoolhouse was finished, only $70 remained in the treasury. The trustees employed L.G.M. Fletcher to teach for two months at a salary of $35 a month. The number of students swelled to 50 or 60 over the next few years, and in the 1860s, when the log cabin could no longer contain all of the students, rooms in the community were rented for the overflow.

In 1867 the log cabin was torn down and replaced by a two-story brick building, which was named the Union School. It opened in the fall of 1867 with seven teachers. That $15,000 building was demolished in 1919 to make way for a larger and more modern school on the same site in the 200 block of North Broad Street. When the residential area that Union School served gave way to commercial use and a larger population of older people in apartments, it was abandoned for school purposes. The handsome building was remodeled into an attractive office complex called Union Square.

As the city's population swelled and spread through the valley, additional public schools were built to service new neighborhoods. In 1871 the Pleasant Grove elementary school was built at Byron and Pleasant streets. The Franklin grade school at Broad and Lafayette streets opened in 1875, and the West Mankato School at West Sixth and Owatonna streets started classes in 1885.

The need for secondary education also was pressing, and Mankato High School at Hickory and South Fifth streets was built and opened in 1891. An addition was added a few years later, and the enlarged building housed students from all parts of the city from grades 7 through 12.

Disaster struck in July 1941 when the old "brick pile," as many called the venerable high school, burned like tinder the morning after summer classes had been completed. Efforts to build a permanent new campus had to wait until after World War II, and then there was a protracted debate and three citywide votes before Mankatoans settled on a $795,000 bond issue to erect the school on Memorial Field. Construction in the area known as the "slough" did require expensive piling as well as much drainage and landfill, but (if much of Chicago could be built on piles so could a school in Mankato) the magnificent structure was open for classes in September 1951, and the scars of battle healed quickly. Even this sparkling new campus, however, was not large enough in the late 1950s after the consolidation of Mankato's school district with those of North Mankato and several rural districts. Enrollment in the consolidated district and pre-school census figures indicated that a second high school would soon be needed. A site on Hoffman Road on the east side of Mankato was selected, and a new $8-million high school was opened in September 1973. The school board named the new school Mankato East and the older school Mankato West, and a friendly cross-

*L.G.M. Fletcher was one of Mankato's earliest settlers and most prominent citizens. Known as "Mr. Education," he was the first teacher in the log cabin school, which opened in 1855. Courtesy, Blue Earth County Historical Society*

town rivalry has since developed between the two high schools.

Parochial schools followed the same growth pattern as did public schools. St. Peter and Paul's Church, which opened the first Catholic school in 1865, built a high school in 1876 and named it Loyola. The School Sisters of Notre Dame, who taught children at St.

*This one-room log cabin, erected in 1855, was Mankato's first public school. L.G.M. Fletcher taught 37 pupils the first year at a salary of $35 a month. Courtesy, Blue Earth County Historical Society*

*As Mankato's population grew, the need for a second public elementary school necessitated building the Pleasant Grove School at Pleasant and Byron streets. Seen here are students gathered for a photo in 1871. This school was replaced by the Lincoln building in 1923. Courtesy, Blue Earth County Historical Society*

Peter and Paul's parish, were offered land on a prominent hilltop just outside the northern city limits, established their Northwest Province there and opened Good Counsel Academy, a boarding school for girls which served Catholics in the immediate Mankato area. Because of sharply falling enrollment, the sisters closed the academy in 1980 and sold the facility to Loyola High School, which moved its entire campus there. The Fitzgerald Middle School, named for a beloved bishop of the Winona Diocese, remained at the site of the old Loyola campus on North Fifth Street. St. Peter and Paul's grade school was relocated to 110 North Sixth Street.

The Immanuel Lutheran Church school has operated continuously since 1867. The first building at Broad and Washington streets was vacated when a new school at 421 North Second Street, adjoining the church, was built. The school expanded to include high-school grades in 1959.

The newer St. John's parish built a substantial stone building in 1947 and opened an elementary school. St. Joseph the Worker parish in West Mankato started its grade school in 1958. Because of ever-increasing costs, a shortage of sisters trained for teaching, and falling enrollment, St. John's school closed in 1973 and merged with

St. Joseph's school. Other parochial schools were Holy Rosary in North Mankato, Mount Olive Lutheran on Marsh Street in East Mankato, St. Mark's Lutheran in West Mankato, and Grace Christian in the prairie district of Mankato, which opened in 1971 and expanded to kindergarten through 12th grade in 1977.

Several church-operated child-care centers served the Mankato area, as did a Headstart program and three privately sponsored preschools. Another church-related school was Bethany Lutheran College, a landmark on the hill overlooking the bend of the river and downtown Mankato. Its roots went back to 1911 when the main building was erected to house a young women's seminary.

In 1927 a small group of pastors and laymen purchased the seminary and presented it to the Norwegian Synod, later the Evangelical Lutheran Synod, for the education of young men and women. Bethany operated as a co-educational high school and junior college until 1969 when the high school department was closed. Bethany Lutheran Theological Seminary became part of the campus in 1947. In 1989 Bethany had 305 students from 16 states and two foreign countries. The new S.C. Ylvisaker Fine Arts Center was completed early in 1990.

State-subsidized higher education first came to Mankato to fill the need for teachers. In 1868 Minnesota's second normal school was founded in Mankato. First teacher diplomas were

*Shown here is the Franklin Grade School, which was built in 1875 on North Broad Street. In 1929 it was replaced by the new Franklin Grade School and Junior High. Courtesy, Blue Earth County Historical Society*

*Elementary education wasn't enough for the children of Mankato, so the district opened its first high school building in 1891. With an addition built a few years later, the high school enrolled all public school students from grades seven through twelve until a fire completely destroyed the entire structure in July 1941. Courtesy, Blue Earth County Historical Society*

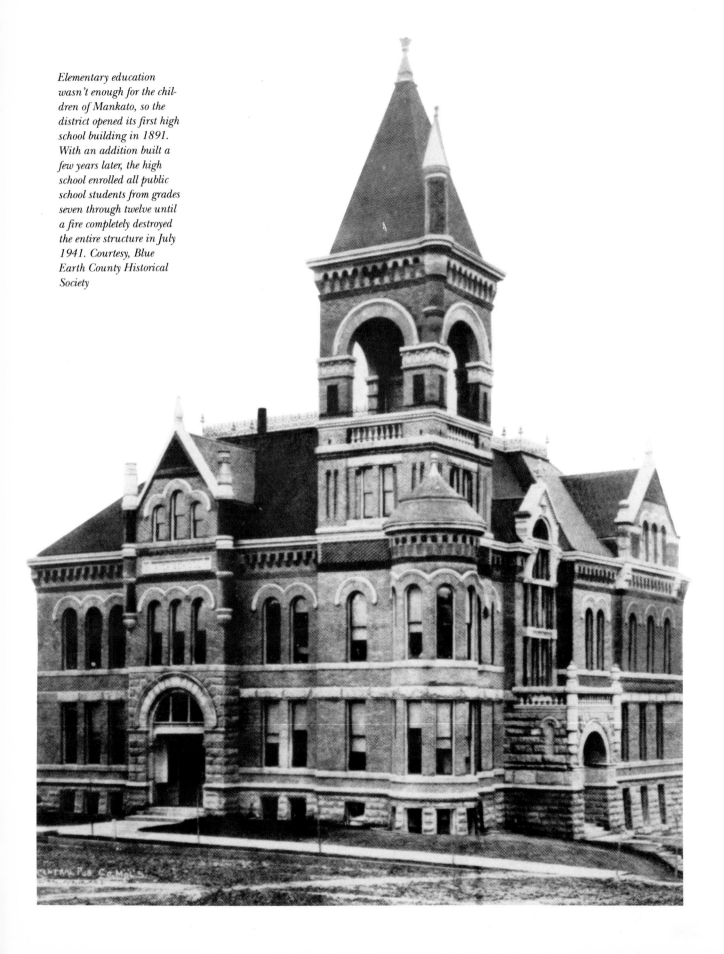

awarded in 1869. But it was not until 1916 that a high school diploma was required for admission.

Beginning in 1921 the state normal schools gained greater stature when they became state teachers colleges. In 1922 the original classroom building was destroyed by fire but in a short time classes were meeting in church basements, lodge halls, and other available rooms in the community. A new and larger building rose from the ashes of the old in 1924. This building, which was later abandoned, was listed in the National Historic Register, and became known as Old Main. It was remodeled into an apartment complex for senior citizens.

While the preparation of teachers continued to be its major role, the mission of Mankato Teachers College, or "TC," as the school was called by two generations of Mankato residents, gradually shifted toward the arts and sciences. The end of World War II brought a flood of veterans to Mankato TC under the GI Bill. Many were more interested in the sciences and business than in education. In 1957 the state legislature recognized the broader mission of the teachers colleges and they became state colleges. Although some former students and townsfolk still called it Mankato TC, the school officially became Mankato State College.

Because there was no more open space for building in the original valley campus area, state officials decreed that

*The School Sisters of Notre Dame came to Mankato in 1865 and began teaching in the St. Peter and Paul's Catholic School. Loyola High School opened in 1876, and is shown here alongside the Loyola Club, a social center. The high school was rebuilt after fires destroyed both structures. Courtesy, Blue Earth County Historical Society*

*TOP: The State Normal School, housed in this building erected in 1870, boosted Mankato's image and strengthened its economy. The stone and brick structure stood on Fifth Street at the head of Jackson Street, overlooking the downtown business district. Courtesy, Blue Earth County Historical Society*

*BOTTOM: With substantial additions to the original building, the State Normal School, seen here around 1880, fulfilled its mission of training teachers. This building was completely destroyed by fire in 1922. A newer and larger structure was built in 1924. Courtesy, Blue Earth County Historical Society*

LEFT: Old Main was completed in 1924 on the site of the State Normal School, which was destroyed by fire in 1922. It was the heart of Mankato State Teachers College (then Mankato State College) and was vacated in 1979 when the hilltop campus was established for Mankato State University. The building, which is on the National Historic Registry, is now a deluxe apartment complex for seniors called Old Main Village. Courtesy, Blue Earth County Historical Society

further expansion of the valley campus would be prohibitive in cost. In 1957 the state acquired 160 acres of land in Mankato's hilltop area for a new campus. The first buildings were erected and in use by 1959, and others were added from year to year.

In 1975 Mankato State College became Mankato State University. Four years later the valley campus was vacated, and the split-campus era of 20 years was ended. By 1989 the campus had all the essentials for a university program—multiple classroom buildings, a library, science buildings, a computer center, an administration building, a student union, dormitories, a performing arts center, athletic fields and football stadium, as well as parking lots—on a site that had grown to more than 300 acres. The university's 15,000 students could select from among 125

undergraduate and 76 graduate degrees.

Two other Mankato-area postsecondary schools made their mark in vocational training. The Mankato Commercial College, a private enterprise, was founded in 1891 by J.R. Brandrup and A.G. Mather. Brandrup was principal owner until his death in 1944. In 1946 the Brandrup interests were bought by A.R. McMuller, who operated the college with his son, Keith, until 1980 when the flow of students went to state-supported technical schools. Among these was the Mankato Vocational Technical School, now known as Mankato Technical College. In the late 1940s Congress and the Minnesota legislature earmarked funds for vocational schools to help train returning veterans. The Mankato school survived in temporary quarters until 1967, when a campus was built on a hill in North Mankato. The state financed a $6-million expansion and by 1989 enrollment surpassed 1,500 with a staff of 156 offering 33 courses. Citizen advisory committees assisted the professional staff in each and every field of instruction.

Mankato was one of hundreds of cities across the country to receive a grant from the Andrew Carnegie Foundation to build a public library. The grant of $40,000 came in 1901 on the understanding that the city would furnish the site and contribute $4,000 a year for the library's maintenance. The building was dedicated and the cornerstone laid on July 2, 1902, and the library opened to the public on June 22, 1903.

From 1906 until 1940 Blue Earth County contracted with the city library to provide library services to county residents. In 1940 the Blue Earth County Library was established as a separate entity, although it was still housed in the Carnegie Library. Bookmobile service to other cities in the county started in 1958. The Minnesota Valley Regional Library was formed in 1967 by a merger of libraries in Blue Earth and Nicollet counties. The city of St. Peter joined in 1968 and Sibley County entered in 1975. In the same year Sibley County joined the Minnesota Valley Regional Library to become a part of the Traverse des Sioux Library System, a nine-county library cooperative. A large new library building was dedicated on May 21, 1977. The

original Carnegie library became The Carnegie Arts Center.

The fine arts have contributed to the good life enjoyed in Mankato and North Mankato since their earliest days. A community band was on hand for the arrival of the first train in 1868. The Orpheus Club, a male chorus started in 1914, and the Women's Glee club were long active and sang for countless community banquets and other functions. Those groups eventually gave way to the Riverblenders for men and the Sweet Adelines for women. The Minnesota Valley Chorale presents several classical concerts each year, and a community chorus performs Handel's *Messiah* each Christmas. Other musical groups—orchestras, bands, and choruses—from

schools and churches have kept the sound of music alive in the Minnesota Valley.

While the Mankato Youth Symphony served as a training ground the real centerpiece of the town's musical world was the Mankato Symphony Orchestra, founded by local musicians in 1952. At first the core of the orchestra came from the staff and students of Mankato State College and Gustavus Adolphus college in St. Peter. Faculty members led the orchestra until 1970, when the internationally known Hermann Herz picked up the baton. Over the next 10 years the orchestra made great strides and achieved professional stature.

In recent years the symphony has

*This quad is crowded many times a day when a large part of the Mankato State University enrollment of 16,000 students passes between classes. Courtesy, Mankato State University News Bureau*

*After World War II, federal and state funds were earmarked for vocational schools to help train returning veterans. Several hundred Mankato veterans attended this trade school, shown here in 1945 in the Kline storage building, under the direction of Harold Ostrem and the Mankato public schools. The school moved to its own building in 1951. Courtesy, Mankato Technical College*

offered a series of concerts through the fall and winter months. One of the nation's few women conductors, Diane Pope of Des Moines, Iowa, quickly won the hearts of Mankato music lovers with her musicianship, sparkling personality, selection of works, and ability to secure nationally known artists to appear as soloists. By 1989 the Mankato Symphony Orchestra had 80 players from 11 southern Minnesota counties, making it a truly regional orchestra.

Given this rich musical heritage, it's no surprise that several Mankato musicians have achieved national and international success. Florence Macbeth, known as the "Minnesota Nightingale," was born in Mankato on January 21, 1891. From childhood on, her voice was recognized as a rare gift. She planned to attend Wellesley College, but on a visit there she was invited to sing at an evening party. Yeatman Griffith, a noted voice instructor, was so impressed that he demanded, "Let me have this voice—now!" So Macbeth went with Griffith to

Pittsburgh and began arduous voice training. Griffith took her to Italy for further training and finally introduced her to audiences in Paris and London, where she proved a sensation. She also sang the role of Gilda in *Rigoletto* in Darmstadt, Germany, where she gained further acclaim.

Back in America Macbeth joined the Chicago Opera Company and starred for six years in *Rigolletto*. The *Chicago Herald Examiner* declared her "one of the greatest of all coloraturas." She also was in demand as a concert singer across the country. She returned to Mankato occassionally and sang with the Orpheus Club. After her death on May 5, 1966, her remains were brought home to Mankato and interred in the Glenwood cemetery.

Two other Mankato natives, Madge Cowden Weeks and Molly Regan, studied voice in New York and sang professionally on the stage. Regan also scored a hit with home folks as soloist with the Mankato Symphony Orchestra in 1988.

Some Mankato artists also have

*Florence Macbeth, an international coloratura opera and concert singer, autographed this photo for a girlhood friend, Maud Hart. Hart also became nationally known as Maud Hart Lovelace, writer of the Betsy-Tacy stories. Courtesy, Blue Earth County Historical Society*

won wide acclaim for their work. Foremost among them was Gilbert Fletcher. Son of L.G.M. Fletcher, one of Mankato's distinguished pioneers, Fletcher perfected the process of linoleum block printing on many materials, including silk, satin, linen, velvet, and mohair, and created prints for framing and wall hanging. His work was featured in *Ladies Home Journal* and other publications. Fletcher also was recognized as a gifted poet. His career was cut short when he died at the age of 50.

Paintings by Mankato nature and wildlife artist Marian Anderson have won numerous honors. Dan Smith had a duck painting selected for a commemorative United States postage stamp in 1987. One of his works also was selected

*The Grand on Front Street in downtown Mankato was one of two long-lived and popular motion picture houses that existed long before Al Jolson starred in "The Jazz Singer" and launched the era of talking pictures. Also showing first-run pictures was the State Theater on Walnut Street, which had its own pit orchestra for a number of years. Courtesy, Blue Earth County Historical Society*

for an Australian stamp.

Mankato's love of theater was evident in the city's early years when the Harmonia Hall was built in 1872 for local and professional productions. The hall burned down in 1882 and was replaced by the Opera House, later called the Orpheum Theater. Mankato's location on the Omaha railroad made it a convenient stop for players on the Orpheum circuit to stop for midweek performances between weekend bookings in St. Paul and Omaha. This brought many famous actors to the Mankato stage. With the arrival of motion pictures, the Orpheum slowly died and the venerable structure was razed in 1931 to make way for an office building.

Theater has stayed alive in Mankato, however, thanks to the Drama

Guild at Mankato State University and student productions at Bethany College and Mankato East, Mankato West, and Loyola high schools. Merely Players, a community organization, gives several performances each season. In addition, the Children's Theater and the Mankato Ballet Company get the youngsters involved in the fun. The Mankato State University Drama Guild also presents plays in the Fine Arts Center, which was once the Carnegie library.

Mankatoans' propensity to organize was not limited to the arts. Women's study clubs that got started early were the Tourist Club (1892), the Clio Club (1892), the Art History Club (1896), and the Zetetic Club (1896). Only the Clio Club has disbanded. By the 1980s there were several garden

*Ladies of this art club watch one of their members putting final touches on a canvas featuring white doves. The group, pictured here around 1900, probably was the forerunner of the Art History Club. Courtesy, Blue Earth County Historical Society*

clubs, three PEO (Philanthropic Educational Organization) chapters for women, as well as chapters of the Association of American University Women, the League of Women Voters, and the Business Women's Club.

Many fraternal organizations also go back to the early years of the two cities. The oldest of these is the Masonic Lodge, chartered in 1856 with George Maxfield as the first master. Other lodges that have been active for many years included the Knights of Columbus, the Elks, the Eagles, the Moose, the Odd Fellows, the Knights of Pythias, and the Foresters. The Elks, Eagles, and Moose lodges have well-appointed dining rooms and clubhouses.

Service clubs have long been active in Mankato. Modern-day Mankatoans can choose among five Kiwanis clubs, three Lions clubs, two Rotary clubs, two Exchange clubs, two Ser-

toma clubs, a Zonta Club for women, Jaycees, Jaycee Women, Toastmasters, and the YMCA. Both the YMCA and YWCA have many activities for families and singles of all ages.

Active forces in the community are Lorentz Post Number 11 of the American Legion and the Veterans of Foreign Wars (Walter H. Strand Post Number 950 and Morson-Ario Post Number 9713). All have strong auxiliaries and excellent club facilities. The national auxilliary of the American Legion was born in Mankato in 1919. Dr. Helen Hughes Hielscher, whose husband, Dr. Julius A. Hielscher, served 16 months in France during World War I, proposed that wives and mothers of veterans could assist the posts in projects to benefit disabled veterans and activities to foster American patriotism. Her ideas received the endorsement of the Minnesota American Legion in 1920

*Many citizens protested loudly the planned destruction of the O.W. Schmidt mansion to make way for a new Y.M.C.A. building, but to no avail. The mansion, one of Mankato's architectural best, was constructed between 1923 and 1925 on a prominent rise from South Front Street in the area called West Mankato. Courtesy, Blue Earth County Historical Society*

and quickly spread nationwide. At Dr. Helen Hielscher's insistence, poppies sold on Poppy Day for the benefit of veterans hospitals and homes, were made solely by veterans themselves.

The success of the 1976 Bicentennial celebration, and particularly the spectacular street parade, prompted formation of a committee to develop an annual celebration in July. The Bend of the River Days was adopted as a name and North Mankato joined the activities by holding its Fun Days on the same dates. The Bend of the River queen, who must be a senior citizen, is crowned along with a band concert and fireworks display at Blakeslee Field on the university campus on July 4 and rides in grand style in the Bend of the River parade a day or two later. Another major event is the Mdewakanton Pow Wow held at the Land of Memories Park, a sacred spot for Indians. Each year in September several hundred

Native Americans gather for traditional dances, ceremonials, and displays.

During the Christmas season thousands of people come to enjoy the Celebration of Lights. Public buildings and businesses are lit up from Thanksgiving to New Years Day. Spectacular residential decorations are put up throughout the community, particularly in the Mary Circle area in North Mankato and the North Broad Street area in Mankato. Traffic on some streets has to be restricted to one way to keep it flowing smoothly every evening. For year-round recreation, Mankato boasts 35 parks of various sizes covering 689 acres. North Mankato has 20 park areas covering 155 acres. Sibley Park, Mankato's largest, was purchased by the city in 1887 and was used as a fairgrounds and race track before being converted to park use. The wild animal zoo was a prime attraction before it was destroyed in the 1965 flood. It was never replaced. Minneopa

State Park, one of Minnesota's oldest, is just outside of Mankato. Its "twice falling water," the English transition of the Indian word Minneopa, has picnic grounds, campsites, and hiking and cross-country ski trails. The historic Seppman stone mill is also a popular spot. Mankato has two outdoor swimming pools—Tourtellotte and Hiniker Pond—and North Mankato has a pool in Spring Lake Park. Indoor pools, open to the public at specified times, are located at Mankato State University's Highland Arena, the YMCA, and Mankato East and West high schools. There are also three golf courses in the community. The Mankato Golf Club is a private membership club. The Terrace View and Minneopa

courses also are privately owned, but are open to the public.

The summer recreation program, organized through the Mankato Area Recreational Council and the public school district, involves 250 softball teams, and there are men's and women's seasonal leagues for volleyball and basketball. A youth baseball association sponsors Little League teams and leagues for older youth groups as well. In 1988 North Mankato finished one of the finest softball facilities in the state. The complex had four lighted diamonds with bleachers built around a central building. The park attracted numerous softball tournaments and a national tournament is scheduled for

*Organized in 1868, the Mankato YMCA erected this building in 1906. It included a swimming pool, a gymnasium, a social hall with kitchen, meeting rooms, a game room, and dormitory rooms for young men. Courtesy, Blue Earth County Historical Society*

*This drum and bugle corps, sponsored by Lorentz Post No. 11 of the American Legion, earned state and national acclaim. After winning numerous state honors, the corps won second place in the national American Legion parade in 1926. The Indian costumes with genuine bonnets and beading were made by Nora Reedfield in her nationally known costume shop in Mankato. Reedfield accompanied the corps to parades and exhibitions to make repairs as needed. Courtesy, Blue Earth County Historical Society*

1990. The area was named Caswell Park in honor of Bud Caswell, a long-time softball and baseball enthusiast who served as public announcer for thousands of games.

In winter the All Seasons Arena near the university campus, schedules hockey games for Mankato State and a team made up of players from Mankato East, Mankato West, and Loyola high schools. Ice time is also scheduled for the public and for the Mankato Figure Skating Club, which stages an annual Ice Revue. There are several outdoor hockey rinks and recreational rinks in Mankato and North Mankato. Mount Kato attracts ski enthusiasts from a wide area with 17 downhill trails, 5 quad chairlifts, and 3 double chairlifts. Snow-making machines keep the 17 runs well surfaced for a long season. The Caledonia Curling Club has indoor rinks for

the winter season and bonspiels in the ancient Scottish game.

Youth activities also include Boy Scouts, Girl Scouts, Camp Fire, and 4-H. The Boy Scouts of America was chartered by Congress in 1910, as was Camp Fire. There were a few scattered Boy Scout units in the are at that time, but not until the Minnesota Valley Area Council was organized in 1927 under the leadership of the Lions Club did the program involve large numbers. The Minnesota Valley Council and the Cedar Valley Council, with headquarters at Albert Lea, merged to create a new Twin Valley Council that served 11 counties. The new council operates Camp Cuyuna, a wilderness reservation near Cross Lake, Camp Norseland near St. Peter, and Camp Cedar Point near Fairmont. The council headquarters and service center are located in Mankato.

Mankato has played a significant role in the National Camp Fire, formerly called Camp Fire Girls. May Fletcher, a Mankato public school-teacher, was the founder of the Camp Fire in Mankato and directed the movement from 1915 to 1946. She was the author of the National Camp Fire *Book of Ceremonials of the Seven Crafts.* Another prime mover for Camp Fire was Ruth Schellberg who served the Mankato Council in many capacities for many years. She was particularly known for guiding wilderness canoe trips in the Canadian border area. Elizabeth Strom, another Mankato teacher, was summer camp director for both Mankato and Fairmont before being chosen as executive director of Camp Fire in St. Paul. From there she went on to become the national camping director for Camp Fire. In 1981 Dr. Margaret Preska, president of Mankato State University, was elected the National Camp Fire board of directors and became national president in 1985.

With Camp Fire so firmly entrenched, the Girl Scouts have a few units in the area, mostly affiliated with

ABOVE: *Dr. Helen Hughes Hielscher was loved and revered for her work as a physician and is remembered today as the founder of the American Legion's National Auxiliary. Courtesy, Blue Earth County Historical Society*

LEFT: *The outdoor pageant staged in Sibley Park in 1916 featured costumes, songs, and dances by ethnic groups who were early settlers in the Minnesota Valley. Courtesy, Blue Earth County Historical Society*

the Peace Pipe Council, which have the Singing Hills camp near Elysian. The 4-H Club movement, founded in Minnesota by T. A. "Dad" Erickson, had several clubs in Mankato.

The people of Mankato and North Mankato have also taken care of their senior citizens and needy. There are four nursing homes, for those needing special care, as well as complexes for low-income elders. Government-supported single homes and apartments are available to qualified families. Summit Center, formerly the Newman Center for Catholic students at Mankato State, was acquired by the Mankato Area Senior Citizens, Inc., as a daily gathering place. It offers seniors noon nutritional meals through the Minnesota Valley Action Council, as well as craft and educational projects. Assisting needy families with daily supplies, the

Echo Food Shelf is supported by public donations and is run by volunteers. The Welcome Inn, also supported by churches and individuals, offers emergency shelter for individuals and families. The Mankato Rehabilitation Association, a citizens group, operates the Rehabilitation Center, which affords full-time employment for a large number of retarded and handicapped men and women. Group housing is provided for many of these workers.

Because of its efforts to provide jobs, health welfare, and recreational facilities for its people with citizen participation, Mankato was honored in 1977 by the National League of Cities with the prestigous All America City award. Both Mankato and North Mankato have been designated Minnesota Star Cities for their community development activities.

*Illustrating the contrasting motive power between an early vintage automobile and a pair of oxen, these Mankatoans pose for a photo on their way to the 1912 Mankato Fair. Courtesy, Blue Earth County Historical Society*

# *Mankato: A Regional Medical Center*

The people of Southern Minnesota have traveled to Mankato for medical treatment ever since Dr. Moses R. Wickersham arrived in the town on May 12, 1856. Later that year three more physicians—Dr. William R. McMahan, Dr. William F. Lewis, and Dr. Albon G. Dornberg— started their practices in Mankato. Until these doctors arrived, the sick and injured depended on their neighbors for assistance. Babies were born at home, probably with the help of midwives. The first white girl born in Mankato was Belle Warner, daughter of Mr. and Mrs. T.D. Warner, on February 24, 1854. The first white boy born was Joseph Kron, son of Clement and Johanna Kron, on May 21, 1854. Joseph grew up to be one of Mankato's early prominent merchants.

As the population of Mankato increased, the need for a hospital became apparent. But it wasn't until 1889, 35 years after the first doctors arrived, that the need was partially satisfied.

Colonel John Tourtellotte, a distinguished Civil War veteran who had settled in Mankato, gave the city $8,000 to provide care for the sick and needy. With Dr. J.W. Andrews and Dr. Charles Warner as consultants, the city built a two-story stone hospital on Fourth Avenue just out-

*ABOVE: Colonel John Tourtellotte donated the money for this hospital, which was built on the prairie north of the city in 1888. The city operated the hospital for nine years before the Sisters of the Sorrowful Mother at Marshfield, Wisconsin, were called to take over management. The sisters ran the hospital from 1897 until 1903, when it was closed. Courtesy, Blue Earth County Historical Society*

*LEFT: Colonel John Tourtellotte, a distinguished Civil War veteran, presented the city with $8,000 to build Mankato's first hospital in 1888. Tourtellotte Park at the north end of Broad Street and Tourtellotte Parkway on north Fourth Street were named in his honor. Courtesy, Blue Earth County Historical Society*

side the northern city limits. Because city water and sewage disposal were not available, water was pumped to a tank in the attic of the hospital and piped to taps on the first and second floors.

Operation of the hospital proved a constant drain on the city treasury. Finally, trustees and city officials appealed to the Sisters of the Sorrowful Mother at Marshfield, Wisconsin, to take over operation of the hospital. Four sisters arrived in 1897 and agreed to run the hospital for $1,000 a year. For the first time, the hospital broke even financially, even if some poor patients were given free care. The contract was renewed in 1898, and the sisters continued to run the hospital for five more years before it was closed in 1903.

The sisters, anxious to provide better care, sought to open a hospital within the city where public utilities were available. They bought the large John S. Willard house at North Sixth and Washington streets and opened a hospital there on July 1, 1898. It had the capacity for 22 patients. That arrangement proved temporary and funds were raised to erect a new building designed especially for hospital use.

Grounds for the new hospital on North Fifth Street just below the Willard property were obtained and foundations were laid in the fall of 1898. The building was completed in 1899 and dedicated in December as St. Joseph's Hospital. By 1913 there was an urgent need for more space and a two-story building was extended to connect with the Willard wing. It provided more patient beds, a chapel, an operating room, and a dressing room. The Willard house then was used chiefly as a home for the aged, and in 1937 was converted to a home for the sisters.

In 1925 the sisters proposed a new fireproof addition. Response to a public fund drive was enthusiastic and work was started in June with a cornerstone ceremony on September 8. Dedication and formal opening occurred exactly one year later—on September 8, 1927.

*The Sisters of the Sorrowful Mother were given complete charge of St. Joseph's Hospital when it was opened on North Fifth Street in 1899. Courtesy, Blue Earth County Historical Society*

This gave the hospital complex a total capacity of 142 beds.

That hospital, too, was inconvenient and became obsolete in some respects, so an entirely new hospital was envisioned. Because space in the valley was limited and expensive, the sisters bought land on Garden Boulevard in the hilltop area, where the new hospital was completed in 1953. The five-story building was designed in the shape of a cross with all wings converging at the center. This concept was convenient and improved services in all of the wings.

Paralleling the growth of St. Joseph's was the Immanuel Hospital, founded by the Immanuel Lutheran Church in 1906 with the help of sister congregations in the Mankato area. The church purchased property on North Fourth Street which had been the site of Omaha Railroad buildings, but was returned to the city when the tracks were rerouted along the river. The cost of the land was $2,500. The hospital was partially built with stone from the old Tourtellotte Hospital. The first

building had room for 30 beds and an annex built in 1912 increased capacity to 65 beds.

Originally, the Immanuel Hospital Association membership was restricted to Lutherans affiliated with the same synod, but in 1932 the charter was amended to accept all Lutherans. Immanuel became a community hospital in 1951. A fund drive in 1952 enabled the hospital to build a new wing and remodel the old.

A close relationship developed between Immanuel and St. Joseph's and some special services and facilities were shared. Talk of merging the two led to an agreement to purchase the sisters' interests, close Immanuel, and move it to St. Joseph's on the hilltop, giving Mankato a truly community hospital under the new name Immanuel-St. Joseph's. The merger became official in January 1960.

In 1978 the hospital association secured financing for a $9-million addition and remodeling which included the installation of air conditioning. Another expansion that cost roughly $10 million will be completed in 1990. The main features of the addition are a cancer treatment center rivaling the world-famous Mayo Clinic at Rochester.

With 90 doctors and a staff of 750, Immanuel-St. Joseph's already serves a wide area of Southern Minnesota, and the new addition is expected to attract many more who might otherwise have to go to Rochester or the Twin Cities for specialist care. The hospital also provides monitoring by telephone wires of cardiac patients in hospitals in Le Sueur, Arlington, St. James, Wells, and Sleepy Eye. The staff also shares in the operation of the municipal hospital in Waseca with a

nonprofit association that leases the hospital from the city. Administrators also offer counsel and assistance to small hospitals in the area.

The Mankato Clinic with a medical and surgical staff of 30 doctors, the Orthopaedic and Fracture Clinic with nine specialists, and other independent doctors and medical clinics also add to Mankato's reputation as a medical center. The Psychiatric Clinic has a staff of 18 specialists and the North Ridge Family Medicine Clinic, a group of four doctors, has offices in North Mankato. The 1989 classified directory for the Mankato area lists 70 physicians and surgeons, 50 dentists, 19 chiropractors, 11 optometrists, 10 opticians, 3 physical therapy clinics, 2 osteopaths, and 3 podiatrists. All of these professionals draw patients from a broad area.

As an outgrowth of an eight-year Heart Health education program designed to educate the public on ways to reduce heart disease, volunteers produced a cookbook, *Cooking a la Heart,* which sold more than 15,000 copies in 1989. Continuing Mankato's health theme, a new nonprofit Health Promotion council, directed by Dr. William Manahan and Dr. Charles Lofy, conducts clinics and seminars covering all phases of physical and mental health through all of Southern Minnesota.

*Lutherans of the Mankato community built Immanuel Hospital on North Fourth Street just below St. Joseph's. Some of the stone blocks from the Tourtellotte Hospital were salvaged and used in construction of Immanuel. Courtesy, Blue Earth County Historical Society*

# The River Is Conquered

*In 1951 flood waters inundated North Mankato (the right side of the Minnesota River) and necessitated the evacuation of all residents of the valley part of the city. In West Mankato, upper right of photo, the new Mankato High School became completely isolated as the water backup increased. Courtesy, Mankato Free Press, Photo by Kenneth E. Berg*

For 138 years the Minnesota River has been both a boon and a bane to the Mankato-North Mankato community. Long before the townsite of Mankato was staked out in 1852 by Parsons K. Johnson and Henry Jackson, Indians had used the waterway as a way of travel and explorers had used it to penetrate into the wilderness. Henry H. Sibley, regional director of the American Fur Company, established a trading post at the junction of the Minnesota and Blue Earth rivers near Chief Sleepy Eyes' Dakota Sioux village. Sleepy Eyes warned Johnson and Jackson that the land just below the river junction flooded frequently, so they chose higher ground when they platted the town. Steamboats brought the first settlers and building materials to Mankato and were the main link with St. Paul until the first railroad arrived in 1868. The first recorded flood at the bend of the river occurred in the spring of 1881, after the winter of the big snow, and parts of Mankato were affected. While North Mankato may have been flooded, there were few settlers there in 1881.

In 1908 North Mankato took the precautionary move of building up Webster Avenue as a dike. The dike was strengthened from time to time and contained the high water of 1929. As further protection, Works Progress Administration crews raised and strengthened Webster Avenue in 1936, and when the river reached flood stage in 1944, the dike held again.

Disaster struck in 1951 when the Blue Earth and Minnesota rivers crested at the same time and rushing waters poured over South Avenue, flooding the entire city of North Mankato. All residents of lower North Mankato were evacuated, while Mankato neighbors opened their hearts and homes and took in the evacuees for several weeks until they could return and clean up their ravaged homes. Losses ran into millions of dollars, but no lives were lost.

Floodwaters had poured in behind the Webster Avenue dike but it was still considered the key to flood control. North Mankato citizens approved a bond issue of $60,000 to repair and build a stronger dike. In 1952 the river crested even higher than it had in 1951, but this time higher and stronger dikes protected both Mankato and North Mankato.

Appeals for further help were made to Washington, and the U.S. Army Corps of Engineers studied the problem of Minnesota River Valley floods. Their plans were never carried out, however, as President Dwight D. Eisenhower vetoed the flood-control bill that had included funds for the proposed project.

Congress passed another flood-control bill in 1958, and again the Corps of Engineers formulated plans for alleviating this constant threat. But nothing had been done when another flood surged through the valley in 1965.

*Mankato's downtown business district was solidly established by 1952. A concrete bridge, constructed in 1917, also brought rapid development to North Mankato which had recovered from the disastrous 1951 flood. The bridge was built at a cost of $100,000 and was widened and repaved in the 1970s. Courtesy, Blue Earth County Historical Society*

LEFT: The Mankato side of the river bore the brunt of the 1965 flood. Mankato West High School was isolated and surrounded by flood waters which filled the lower levels of the building. Courtesy, Mankato Public Schools

FACING, BOTTOM: Remembering the disastrous flood of 1951, North Mankato prepared for another in 1965 by sandbagging the Webster Avenue dike. The efforts paid off as North Mankato escaped most of the flood when the Blue Earth River bypassed Sibley Mound and poured down Mound Avenue in West Mankato. Courtesy, City of North Mankato

The lower areas of North Mankato again were evacuated for fear the dikes might not hold. Hundreds of volunteers filled sandbags and manned the dikes as the water rose.

This time North Mankato was spared, but Mankato was hit hard. The Blue Earth River reached record heights and its waters surged through Sibley Park, pouring down Mound Avenue and into the Minnesota and Poplar street area, flooding Madsen's supermarket with four feet of water. Water poured into the "slough" area, flooding lower levels of Mankato High School. However, water did not reach the main downtown district.

The 1965 flood precipitated further action from the Corps of Engineers. Their first recommendation was to construct a high dam from bluff to

bluff across the Blue Earth River. This, they said, would hold back the waters at flood time and thus assure much lower crests in the Minnesota River through Mankato and North Mankato, as well as relieving flood threats to Carver and Chaska farther downstream.

Engineers believed the high dam would protect against the highest flood that might occur once in 300 years. It would have cost millions of dollars and created a reservoir that would have backed water up the Blue Earth Valley, flooding thousands of acres in its tributaries and even reaching the town of Garden City. The uproar from every segment of the population—farmers and townspeople, civic leaders and public officials—was so loud that the plan was aborted.

After further studies, the Corps of

Engineers developed an alternate plan, which included concrete walls and earthen dikes through Mankato and North Mankato and construction of a new bridge between the two cities. The old concrete bridge had to be removed as it might become an obstacle to the flow of ice, fallen trees, and other debris. This plan, the engineers said, should contain the highest flood that might occur once in 100 years. This project was completed and the new bridge was opened to traffic in 1987. It was later dedicated as Veterans Memorial Bridge with fitting pomp and ceremony.

With all fears of further floods virtually eliminated, Mankato and North Mankato are looking to the future. Several hundred volunteers, under a multifaceted ACT 2000 organization, are charting community direction as the community approaches the year 2000. They aim to come up with an overall plan for making the area a most favorable and vibrant place to live with a strong economic climate.

Replacing previous community development organizations—Come to Mankato, Mankato Area Promotion, and the Mankato Industrial Development Corporation—the new Valley Development Corporation evolved in 1983. In 1986 the Valley Venture Club raised over a million dollars earmarked for the development of enterprises that would contribute to the economy of the greater Mankato and North Mankato community. The bend of the river communities are optimistic and excited over their future as 1990 ushers in a new decade of cooperation.

*ABOVE: Farming of the important staple crop soybean takes place near North Mankato. Photo by Joe Miller*

*RIGHT: In the Sioux language "Minneopa" means "twice falling water." Minneopa State Park, five miles west of Mankato, has two waterfalls (seen here is the upper falls). The 11,000-acre park offers cross country skiing in the winter and camping and picnicking in the summer. Photo by Joe Miller*

*The late day sun highlights horses grazing at the foot of Good Counsel hill. The pasture, which is property of Mankato Province at the School Sisters of Notre Dame, is rented out to Mankato residents and their horses. Photo by Joe Miller*

*ABOVE: At the convergence of the Blue Earth and the Minnesota rivers, in the sacred spot called Land of Memories Park, a traditional Native American powwow takes place each September. The reunion gathers together Native Peoples from all over the United States who come to celebrate their heritage and keep traditions alive. Photo by Joe Miller*

*RIGHT: The Mankato Mdewakaton Powwow festivities include colorful ceremonial dances, crafts, and food. Traditions are also passed on. Including Mankato residents, the event draws about 5,000 people. Photo by Joe Miller*

*LEFT: Nestled among the trees in Sibley Park is one of Mankato's first log dwellings, the Ott Cabin. Built in 1857 and originally located in Mankato township, the cabin was moved to Sibley Park in 1931. Photo by Gregg Andersen*

ABOVE: By far the biggest recreational lake visited by Mankatoans is Lake Washington. Just a few miles northeast of the city, residents can get away and enjoy water-skiing, sailing, sailboarding, and great fishing. Photo by Gregg Andersen

RIGHT: Each summer the Kato Cycle Club holds several motocross races, including hill climbs and hare scramblers. Photo by Joe Miller

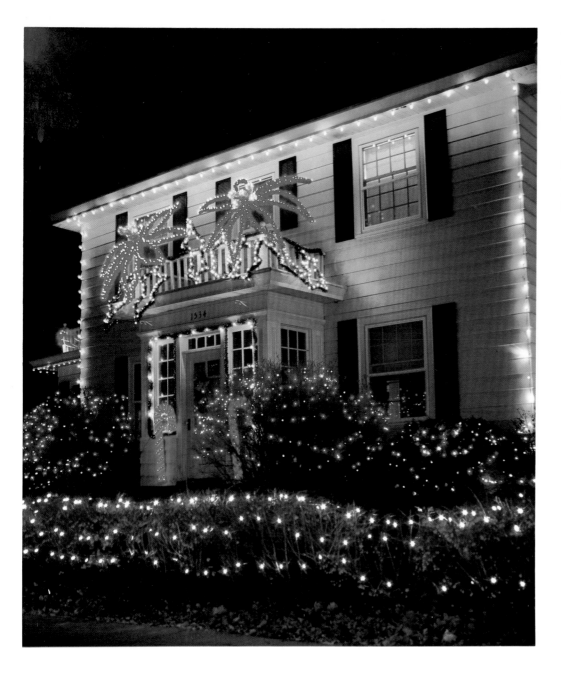

*Each Christmas season thousands of people come to enjoy the Celebration of Lights in Mankato and North Mankato. Public buildings and businesses are illuminated from Thanksgiving to New Year's Day. This spectacular residence is located on North Broad Street in Mankato. Photo by Deneve Feigh Bunde*

Mankato has had countless baseball teams, but the
1889 Baltics were unique—they had the first pitcher in
these parts who kept batters fanning the air with his
curve ball. He was Billy Mead, seen here reclining,
front left. Courtesy, Blue Earth County Historical
Society

# *Partners In Progress*

Parsons Johnson and Henry Jackson were at the rail of the steamer *Yankee* in 1850. Townsite fever and dreams of monetary gain were no doubt on their minds as the *Yankee* left St. Paul and later negotiated the big bend of the Minnesota River to an Indian encampment at the confluence with the Blue Earth River, today's Sibley Park. This sector of Dakota Indian territory was opened up to white settlers with the impending signing of the Treaty of Traverse des Sioux in 1850.

Mankato as a townsite came into being in February 1852. North Mankato, on what had been a floodplain, was platted in 1857 and incorporated in 1899.

The Mankato area was a trade center from its inception.—"Customers coming as far away as Iowa," a newspaper headline of the late 1850s read.

The railroads did not arrive until 1868. The Minnesota River was the original principal avenue of transport of masses of people, raw materials, and machinery to what then was America's midwestern frontier.

Agriculture was predominant. Wheat and corn were planted and harvested in abundance on the rich soil. And farming was supported by a multitude of milling and retailing establishments.

Within the growing community came a demand for education.

And with this enlightenment there were homegrown industries that first served local needs, and later grew to meet national and international markets.

But beyond agriculture and public education, no single industry dominated Mankato/North Mankato. The strength of the cities over the decades is the diversity in the marketplace. The national economy may rise and fall, but Mankato/North Mankato will not be fractured.

With the floods of 1951 and 1965, Mankato and North Mankato began to realize that they were in things together. The "Greater Mankato area" began to have more homogenous meaning. It represents an impressive service area with a 60-mile radius.

Educational, commercial, medical, legal, technical, transport, and recreational interests were the Mankato area's challenge a century ago. It is no different today.

Mankato/North Mankato's institutions of higher learning have record enrollments. City governments are vigorous in law enforcement, fire protection, and the pursuit of new business, shopping malls, and industry.

In the past, Native Americans skirted Mankato/North Mankato on their drives across the state. From their perspective, they did not feel welcome there after the retaliatory hanging of 38 Sioux in December 1862 following the summer's uprising. But today a Native American powwow is an annual September feature in a park dedicated to Mankato's original inhabitants.

Mankato/North Mankato owes its present and future to a reconciliation of Native Americans and European settlers, a landscape rich in historical background, fertile soil, a commitment to education, soundly operated family-owned businesses, and industrial innovation.

The businesses, organizations, and institutions whose histories are detailed on the following pages have chosen to support this significant literary and civic project. The involvement of Mankato/North Mankato residents in business and local government has helped to make the community an excellent place in which to live, work, and raise families.

# MANKATO AREA CHAMBER OF COMMERCE

Mankato's industrial and merchandising community had grown rapidly by 1868, 16 years after the city's founding. As a result, area businesses banded together in the expectation of consolidation and further expansion of the competitive marketplace.

The Mankato Board of Trade was thus organized September 11, 1868, with John Barr as the first president. In about 1900 the organization's name was changed to Mankato Commercial Club, reflecting the infusion of more consumer services brought about by modernization. In 1920 its name was changed again to the more encompassing Mankato Chamber of Commerce. Ed Nyquist and E.F. Rogers were prominent in directing the chamber's more formative years during the 1930s and 1940s.

Roger Nygaard, the chamber's seventh executive director, says, "Today the chamber's emphasis is people—people working together to solve the socioeconomic challenges of our community. Business and professional men and women have a common interest and pride in their community. The chamber is a vehicle that enables people to meld their divergent interests into a cohesive force, to build a better place, and to develop better citizenship."

The current chamber of commerce embraces Mankato, North Mankato, and the suburbs of Skyline and LeHillier. The association has 675 members and has 10 standing, active committees: area retail, agriculture, business activities, governmental affairs, housing, solicitations, transportation, hospitality, ambassadors, and presidents club.

A Convention and Visitors Bureau was opened in 1984. The chamber provides administrative, eight-member staff services and related support to other affiliates' programs unheard of in 1868. They

*In 1966 The Mankato Area Chamber of Commerce left its longtime offices at Walnut and South Second streets (above) to move to a higher visibility site in the heart of the business area on South Front Street (right). When urban renewal claimed the building in 1975, the chamber moved to a large second-story suite in the nearby Martin Building.*

are: Valley Industrial Development Corp., ACT (Active Community Thought) 2000, strategic planning, Southern Minnesota Highway Improvement Association, Leadership Mankato Area, Mankato Area Foundation, Bend of the River Festival, Service Corps of Retired Executives (SCORE), North Mankato Civic and Commerce Association, Airport Commission, and Region 9 Industrial Safety Council.

The Mankato Area Chamber of Commerce continues to welcome new businesses to the area with its first dollar of profit—a one-dollar bill enclosed in a glass-faced frame on the wall.

# REGAN, REGAN & MEYER

The law firm of Regan, Regan & Meyer traces its origin to 1910, when John E. Regan, then a first-year attorney, moved his office and family from southwestern Minnesota to Mankato.

John Regan became well known as an aggressive and innovative trial lawyer in south-central Minnesota. He also acquired a statewide reputation in the 1930s as a feisty politician. Regan was gregarious and articulate. He served one term in the state legislature and gained his party's nomination for governor and the U.S. Senate.

Other Mankato lawyers who became associated with Regan before establishing their own individual practices include B.D. Grogan, for four years in the late 1920s; Arthur J. Berndt (later a North Mankato municipal judge), for three years in the mid-1930s; and Kenneth Krost (later a Mankato city attorney), for two years in the 1930s.

Regan's son, Robert M. Regan, born in Mankato in 1911, was admitted to the bar in the District of Columbia in 1937 and in Minnesota two

*Founder John E. Regan (left) discusses matters with a client in his first Mankato office, circa 1915.*

years later. He returned to Mankato to join his father in the law firm, which then became Regan & Regan. In 1940 Robert Regan was federal district director of the census. Father and son were close associates, primarily as trial lawyers, until the death of John Regan in 1946.

Robert Regan continued alone, still emphasizing trial law until 1949, when H. Clifton Kroon, a Mankato native newly admitted to the bar, became a partner. Regan & Kroon was a general practice entity until 1966.

Robert Regan and Cliff Kroon were also entrepreneurs. With the advent of television and acknowledging Mankato's distance from telecasting stations and its location in a sunken, river valley, they founded the first community cable antenna system in Minnesota, in the early 1950s. They constructed a dozen other cable systems in southern Minnesota, remaining as owner/operators of the Mankato/North Mankato system un-

til 1965 and of the New Ulm system until 1989. Robert Regan was recognized as a "pioneer" in Minnesota cable television by the National Cable Television Association in 1967.

Robert's son, John E. "Jack" Regan, born in Mankato in 1940, became the third generation of Regans to be admitted to the bar and to become associated with the family practice. Licensed as a certified public accountant (CPA) in 1965 and as a lawyer in 1967, Jack brought to the firm a dimension of business and tax law. Another of Robert's sons, R. Michael Regan, also practiced with his father and brother from 1972 to 1979 as a trial lawyer.

Daniel H. Meyer, holding lawyer and CPA credentials similar to Jack Regan's, joined the firm in 1974, amplifying the firm's continuing concentration in business and tax law.

In June 1989 Robert Regan received the Senior Counselor Award from the Minnesota State Bar Association, in recognition of his 50 years of service as a lawyer in Minnesota.

The firm moves into its 81st year with lawyers Robert Regan, Jack Regan, and Dan Meyer dedicated to downtown Mankato, their offices (now in Mankato's newest office building, the Heco Building) still located less than a block from the original one-man site on South Front Street occupied by the senior John E. Regan in 1910.

*LEFT: John E. Regan in the 1930s. His was a familiar face on political campaign posters.*

*RIGHT: Robert M. Regan, trial lawyer and cable television pioneer.*

# THE DOTSON COMPANY

The Dotson Company had its beginnings in 1876, when Lawrence Mayer opened a blacksmith shop on Mankato's Vine Street. Twenty years later Louis, one of his three sons then in the business, invented the powered trip hammer, the mechanical smithy that in various versions would give the firm and successors a national and international reputation. In 1908 the Mayers also designed and produced one of the first V-8 gasoline engines for automobiles. The manufacturing company's lines were expanded to include tractors, road-grading equipment, a complete line of woodworking tools, and even a very successful mechanical clothes-drying line.

But money problems plagued the Mayers. In 1916 stockholders asked them to step down. Commercial banks ran the firm until 1923, when L.J. "Joe" Fazendin was brought in and, in 1937, took ownership.

Ervin "Ed" Dedrickson, Harold Stofferahn, Cliff Fossen, and Lyle Ulman have each been with the organization for more than 40 years. In fact, Dedrickson is the seventh

member of his family to work in the foundry and machine shop, representing more than 200 years of service to the company from one family. Dedrickson and the others endured the lean times and basked in the good years that mark the long history of the firm.

In 1937, during the depth of the Depression, Dedrickson had a part-time job as an apprentice machinist at Little Giant, The Dotson Company's immediate predecessor. Eight hours of work paid one dollar per day.

It was a tenuous relationship, about which Ed was not entirely aware. Little Giant was at the brink of bankruptcy, and the hometown investors wanted out. Joe Fazendin, the plant manager brought in from Canada, had stripped the company of unprofitable product lines (notably farm tractors) to regain profitability. In September 1937 Fazendin courageously purchased the firm's slim assets to go it alone.

"I remember Mr. Fazendin very clearly," says Dedrickson. "Joe was doing his best to keep the company alive."

Little Giant and Ed Dedrickson survived the Depression. Dedrickson was hired full time in 1939, as clouds of World War II hovered. "I was made a machinist at 25 cents an hour," recalls Dedrickson. "My paycheck for the week was $11.88— 12 cents having

*Employees of Mayer Bros., The Dotson Company's predecessor, celebrate the Fourth of July aboard a parade float, adorned with machine shop equipment. Photo circa 1900*

been deducted for Social Security."

Little Giant Co. expanded vastly during the war years. It forged many metal products for the military effort. But its most prominent contribution was a trip hammer—a rigid, upright device that, when activated, shaped metal into prescribed proportions. Little Giant's machines were regarded as the best, and government war specifications soon required "Little Giant or equal" quality.

A great motivator during this period was Fazendin's son-in-law, Jerry Dotson, brought into the firm in 1943. "Jerry was a fine person," says Dedrickson. "You could talk to him. He made you feel good. I was never out of a job; there were no layoffs. My wife and I later had three daughters, and we had a comfortable life. I looked around at my friends and realized I was better off than many of them.

"Sure, we had bad moments. I didn't particularly like getting out of bed at midnight, especially on a Sunday, when there was a breakdown. But it went with the job."

As the foundry expanded and the manufacturing lines diminished, the name of the firm was changed from Little Giant to The Dotson Company. Jerry Dotson continued to over-

*Dotson predecessor Mayer Bros. produced this Little Giant oil (diesel-powered) farm tractor in 1914.*

*Dotson made an active contribution to the war effort with production of the Little Giant trip hammer, shown here being produced at the plant circa 1943.*

see a steady growth of the organization until his death in 1978.

But favorable economic times were not destined to last forever at The Dotson Company. The employees would have to live through one more trauma.

In 1982 the firm lost 80 percent of its business because of the economic downturn following the fuel crises of the 1970s. The company, which had boomed with frantic oil exploration, was skidding because of demobilization of drilling rigs after fuel surpluses evolved. Agriculture, too, was in a recession, and farmers were not buying new equipment or were putting off repairs.

The machine shop where Dedrickson worked was shut down. This tough medicine was followed by the closing of the aluminum, brass, and steel casting departments. From then on, The Dotson Company would be strictly an iron foundry.

Harold Stofferahn joined the firm in 1943. He became a supervisor in 1958 and is now plant manager. "One machine today can do what 10 people used to do," Stofferahn says. "But people still make up the company—and the quality of the people makes my job easier."

Stofferahn was there with others in 1982, when Dennis Dotson, Jer-

ry's son, emulated his grandfather's 1937 drastic reduction of the company's exposure to expenses, in order to survive. "Not only were departments shut down," Stofferahn says, "but employees had to absorb 45-percent pay cuts. And all showed up—yes, some grumbling—for work the next day."

Cooperative labor, sensitive management, mechanization, electric furnaces, increased productivity (400 percent), cyclical good luck, and a revived economy combined to benefit the company.

Dennis Dotson is gratified that the last "pay" certificates given to employees in lieu of lost compensation were redeemed in 1988.

"We're so much more modernized and efficient now," says Lyle Ulman, a 49-year employee. "We've been up and down, so I appreciate today's stability." Ulman was hired by Joe Fazendin as an office clerk and for many years supervised all the office functions for the company.

Cliff Fossen has been on the core production line since 1948. "Each of our four automatic molding machines can make more castings in one hour than what one person used to in one day." Fossen remembers the time when all the sand cores were made by hand and had to be baked for hours before they were hard enough to put into the molds. Today many of the cores are made on large machines, and the processes have eliminated the baking so

that they may be used immediately.

Whereas half of the nation's 1,500 iron foundries shut down furnaces since 1980, The Dotson Company today is meeting its $10-million-per-year capacity. In the hands of plant manager Harold Stofferahn is the current capacity expansion plan that will take the company to $14-million sales level for the 1990s.

The economic travails that followed the 1970s tested the strength of all the employees. But, as in 1937, The Dotson Company has rallied, and now it faces the 1990s as a market leader, serving national customers such as Toro, Rockwell, and John Deere, and local manufacturers typified by MICO and Kato Engineering.

For the past 100 years, The Dotson Company's employees have made the difference between success and potential failure. While the ownership has transferred from the Mayers to the banks to the Dotsons, the real soul of the firm has remained constant with people such as Ed Dedrickson, Harold Stofferahn, Lyle Ulman, and Cliff Fossen. They set the example, they teach, and they lead.

*This photograph, circa 1900, shows the original Mayer Bros. foundry, on the same site that The Dotson Company occupies today. Mayer's larger addition can be seen at left.*

# JOHNSON FISHING, INC.

If necessity can be the mother of invention, then invention inarguably has been the mother of a flourishing leisure equipment industry in Mankato—Johnson Fishing, Inc.

It started in 1948. Lloyd Johnson, a machinist at Kato Engineering Co., and Warren Denison, a bait shop operator, mused during lake outings that there ought to be a way to devise a fishing reel that wouldn't backlash, creating snarls and delays that can take some of the fun out of fishing.

The two began casting ideas and, by the following spring, fabricated a prototype closed-face spinning reel from an old alarm clock casing and some hand-forged parts. They showed the device to friends and fished with it. Eventually, with borrowed money, they created the tooling.

Johnson and Denison began hand-assembling the new kind of reel in the Johnson home and took it to sports shows and fishing tackle exhibitions in the Midwest, where it gained immediate acceptance by trade buyers. In 1950 the partners

*Cofounder Lloyd Johnson (right) confers with Gene Menne, chief engineer at Johnson Reels. Inventor of the world-famous Johnson Reel, Johnson registered more than 20 patents, despite being blind for the last 10 years of his life.*

turned out 1,000 of the new Johnson Sidewinder spincast reels and discovered the demand was much greater than that number. By 1970 Johnson Reels, Inc. (the company was originally named Denison-Johnson, Inc.), had produced and marketed millions of Johnson Reels from a handsome new plant. A year earlier the firm had acquired a little-known Moorhead manufacturer of electric trolling motors named Minn Kota.

Warren Denison died in 1958, and Lloyd Johnson had a terminal illness. The expanded company then was acquired by S.C. Johnson and Son, Inc. (the Johnson's Wax people), of Racine, Wisconsin. Additional acquisitions were made regularly to make up what today is Johnson Fishing, Inc. Included are Bass Buster Lures, Johnson Silver Minnow Spoons, Little Stinker Catfish Baits, Mitchell Reels, and CrabClaw Marine anchors.

Johnson Fishing now is a division of Johnson Worldwide Associates, Inc., a publicly held company that was spun off from Johnson's Wax in 1986. Johnson Fishing products are sold in North America, South America, Europe, Asia, and Africa. Its Minn Kota motors have become the world market leader in that category, and its early fishing reel products are in the Freshwater Fishing Hall of Fame in Hayward, Wisconsin.

Johnson Fishing in Mankato employs nearly 300 people in 170,000 square feet of manufacturing space. An additional 150 workers

are employed at its permanent magnet motor plant in Racine and its fishing lure operations in Amsterdam, Missouri. Ward R. Tenney, president of Johnson Fishing, Inc., says, "We will work every day to do what Lloyd Johnson and Warren Denison did—trying to create products that make fishing more productive and more fun."

*Cofounder Warren Denison poses with two sizable trout brought in by a Johnson Reel.*

*From an old alarm clock casing came the Johnson Reel prototype, fabricated in 1948 by Lloyd Johnson and Warren Denison.*

# HONEYMEAD PRODUCTS COMPANY

It was not a farmer, but a young lawyer, who was most instrumental in the formation of what today is Honeymead Products Company.

William Blethen was handling a legal case in Winona, rooming with a client, Riley Lewis, a retired county extension agent. It was then, in 1938, that Lewis extolled the success of soybeans in his native Iowa. He sent Blethen home with the beginnings of an idea that a soybean-processing plant in Mankato might prosper.

Blethen recruited investors. Of the $50,000 raised, $7,500 was spent to obtain title of the abandoned Minnesota Pipe and Tile Co., a site consisting of several warehouses, a building suitable for offices, railroad tracks, and a block of real estate near the confluence of the Blue Earth and Minnesota rivers. Blethen was a kind of envangelist, exhorting farmers to plant soybeans and to ship their produce to Mankato.

Thus, in 1939, Mankato Soybean Products Inc. was formed. The principal piece of equipment was a single expeller that extracted oil from soybeans purchased from supportive area farmers.

Lewis, who had put the soybean bug in Blethen's ear, was named first plant manager. He was succeeded in 1941 by Ed Ober, a Lake Crystal farmer. Ober fortunately hired Fran Bergemann as a key employee, for it was Bergemann who adapted the plant to also process flax, helping to make the operation profitable.

In 1942 Washington Egg and Poultry Association, a cooperative, purchased the company and operated it until 1949, when it was

---

*At Honeymead Products 80,000 bushels of soybeans are processed each day; 12 railroad cars of refined oil and 18 cars of hydrogenated oil are shipped out daily.*

bought by the Andreas family. The Andreas family had feed mills in Iowa under the name Honeymead, and, as a result, Mankato Soybean Products became known as Honeymead Products Company.

Honeymead's chief officer, Lowell Andreas, introduced revolutionary soybean oil solvent extraction technology from Europe. Whereas before soybeans were crushed to remove the oil, the Andreas' process removed it chemically. The plant was thus refitted several times in the 1950s to keep up with change.

In 1960 Honeymead was sold to the Farmers Union Grain Terminal Association, a St. Paul-based grain marketing terminal. Three years later Honeymead expanded into hydrogenated or hardened soybean oil, the basis for margarine and shortening. In 1968 Lowell Rasmussen was named president and continued the growth initiated by the Andreas family.

Production has expanded markedly in the past 25 years— from 50,000 bushels of soybeans, five railroad tank cars of refined oil, and four tank cars of hydrogenated oil per day, to the present capacity of 80,000 bushels, 12 cars of refined oil, and 18 cars of hydrogenated oil daily.

Rasmussen retired in 1984 and Merritt Petersen succeeded him as president.

Honeymead Products Company and its 185 employees continue to serve Minnesota, the United States, and several foreign countries.

# MANKATO STATE UNIVERSITY

Community support of Mankato State University had its inception before predecessor Mankato Normal School began classes in 1868, 16 years after the city's 1852 founding.

Daniel Buck was a pioneer Mankato attorney, member of the state legislature, and a Minnesota Supreme Court judge. He also became known as the father of the Mankato Normal School system.

Buck was instrumental in a revision of statutes permitting state taxpayer support of normal, or teacher-training, schools. Normal school is a translation of the French phrase *ecole normale,* so named because it was intended to serve as a model school. Mankato would become the second Minnesota site of such an institution, but with a proviso that the town respond and match the legislature's generosity.

Asking for a $5,000 subscription from Mankato businessmen and residents, Buck said, in an impassioned, prophetic 1868 speech: This is not an institution intended for the few, but a state institution where hundreds and ultimately thousands of teachers shall be taught the theory and practice of teaching the children of our state, from whence untold benefits will flow to the door of every citizen, repaying tenfold every dollar invested. It is not Mankato simply that is to be benefited, but entire southwestern Minnesota."

Twenty-seven students enrolled in Mankato Normal's first class in 1868 in rented quarters at the Methodist Episcopal Church. All were from Mankato or the immediate area.

By contrast, 121 years later, in 1989 registrations numbered 14,587 on-campus and 1,728 off-campus students for a total of 16,315. Buck's vision of service to southwestern Min-

*The stately Old Main building, lost to a fire in 1922, serves as a scenic backdrop for a group of students in an 1884 photo.*

nesota had been enlarged to the entire southern half of the state, including the Twin Cities, northern Iowa, and a generous sprinkling of other states and foreign nations.

The Mankato Normal School of 1868 transcended into Mankato State Teachers College in 1921, Mankato State College in 1957, and Mankato State University in 1975. The original one- to two-year curriculum of teacher training was gradually broadened to a rainbow of liberal and fine arts extending to the graduate level.

Whereas the cities of Mankato and North Mankato reaped economic and intellectual dividends from the presence of the halls of higher learning, there would have to be a continued local commitment through the decades. Valuable property was relinquished as the inner-city campus unfolded. Responsibilities of providing utilities and fire and police protection were added. Significant political and lobbying clout was to come from the citizen-sponsored Education Association of Southern Minnesota.

Following two years' temporary

*A vaulting fountain and beautiful trees create a peaceful environment conducive to study at the campus center.*

*Faithfully telling the time for students and staff, the university's bell tower epitomizes the school's new look that began taking shape in the 1970s.*

residence in the historic Shaubut Building, Mankato Normal established itself physically when three-story Old Main was completed on South Fifth Street in 1870. Only 14 subjects were taught then, none straying beyond the basic "3 Rs."

George Gage was Mankato Normal's first principal, succeeded in 1872 by his assistant, Julia Sears. In 1873 a retired Methodist minister, David John, abruptly replaced Sears amid some controversy at the time of the women's suffrage movement.

In 1880 Edward Searing became the school's first head to be called president. His tenure also brought 18 years of expansion and curriculum development. During that period the school began offering courses above the high-school level as well as a five-year instructional program. Two wings were added to Old Main.

Searing was succeeded by Charles Cooper in 1898. A full-size

addition was made to the south side of Old Main to serve as a kindergarten-12th grade laboratory school for would-be elementary-school teachers. The first female dormitory, Daniel Buck Hall, was erected in 1913, followed by Cooper Hall in 1921.

The university experienced near disaster in 1922, when Old Main was destroyed by fire. But the state legislature responded immediately, approving funds for a handsome (and since preserved for senior-citizen housing) replacement in 1924.

In 1930 Frank McElroy became president, the first to hold a Ph.D. degree. In 1934 tuition was charged for the first time, and five years later a modern physical education building was opened. Education of teachers was lengthened to four years of college preparatory work.

Clarence Crawford was named president in 1946 and excelled at successfully blending community support with legislative intent. He and state senator Val Imm were the catalysts in first optimizing Mankato State's confined campus, blueprinting a new hilltop location that was once a cornfield one mile away. Enrollment grew to 9,500 students with a faculty of 450, and the school's athletes won conference and national acclaim.

James Nickerson was president during the tumultuous 1960s and 1970s. Douglas Moore followed during the post-Vietnam War retrenchments, carefully abandoning the old campus and furthering development and expansion of the new. Margaret Preska was chosen the institution's 10th president in 1979.

The broader perspective of community action's educational role in the 1980s and 1990s has been underwritten with a zeal comparable to that of the 1860s. Three buildings of the new campus have been erected with Mankato State Foundation's corporate and individual support, and many student scholarships have been privately funded. An electrical-engineering program introduced in the 1980s exists in large part because of the leadership and support of the community.

Already well into its second century, Mankato State University continues to grow. Its development from a teacher training institution to a seven-college university with a high-technology thrust enriching the region long ago fulfilled Daniel Buck's promise that untold benefits to citizens would repay "tenfold every dollar invested."

*Students prepare to meet the challenges of the high-technology age at Trafton Science Center.*

# AUGUST DEIKE TRANSFER, INC.

Whether August Deike Transfer, Inc., would survive to observe its centennial in 1986 depended on the outcome of Russell Deike's impassioned petition to the state trucking regulatory agency in 1956.

Deike Transfer was at a crossroads. The firm could remain a small local transporter of goods, as it had been since it was founded by Russ Deike's grandfather in 1886, and continue to be an area contract carrier as it had since 1950. But to grow and secure itself financially, Deike would need intrastate access to the major hub of Minneapolis-St. Paul.

The Mankato-Twin Cities motor route had been locked into a monopoly held by a St. Paul firm. Russ Deike, attorneys, unions, and businessmen campaigned for four months to end the exclusivity, saying south-central Minnesota needed a second carrier. Their arguments eventually proved compelling.

Deregulation of the trucking in the early 1980s further propelled Deike Transfer to an established position to serve a greatly expanded market. Today the firm touches 64 cities in Minnesota and 150 in Iowa, operating out of two terminals. Jim Deike does this daily with a fleet of 7 tractors, 12 highway trailers, and 2 small trucks.

"My great-grandfather founded the business, and his son, August Jr., nursed it," says president Jim Deike. "But it was my late father, Russ, who gave it impetus and modern direction."

August Deike, Sr., was a German immigrant who came to Mankato in 1874. He left a job at a flour mill to become a drayage entrepreneur, using horses and wagons to haul general merchandise freight, feed, and seeds from railroad depots to waiting customers. He also moved furniture from house to house.

August Sr. took his three sons into the business. Trucks and vans were replacing horses and wagons, and there was opportunity for both growth and specialization.

A common misconception is that the sons split off to compete against themselves. To the contrary, August Jr. remained with his father to concentrate on the transfer of merchandise, while brothers Ben and Fred set up their own firm to transport and store household goods. They were compatible companies, and the names of August Deike and Ben Deike continue as separate business entities today.

August Jr., who took over from his father in 1927, saw the company through the Depression. He did this in part by expanding his services—notably picking up coal from railroad gondolas and delivering it to homes, businesses, and industries.

When August Jr.'s son, Russ, entered the Navy Seabees during World War II, use of coal was giving way to natural gas. Russ and his

RIGHT: Founder August Deike, Sr., works at his desk, surrounded by telephones and notes at his office at 228R South Front Street in Mankato. Photo circa 1908

BELOW: Russ Deike poses with one of his two trucks in a photograph taken circa 1950.

wife, Betty, would therefore have a further challenge when he doffed his uniform at war's end.

The trucking industry had been state regulated since 1935. Whereas this action brought tighter insurance and safety standards, it also severely constrained Russ and Betty from enlarging the firm's focus. But Russ was determined. First he obtained contract authority in 1950 and the coveted Twin-Cities route six years later. He coined the nickname Deike Trux, boldly stated and highly identifiable on his trucks and letterheads.

Betty Deike, widowed in 1981, remains on the board of directors. Russ and Betty's son, Jim, worked his way up the company ladder. As a boy he did odd jobs and became a rate clerk and a driver. He succeeded his ailing father as president in 1979.

Jim Deike's challenges have been different, but no less formidable. State regulations that had some-

*Coal delivery was an important facet of August Deike Transfer's operations in the 1930s, as evidenced by the illustration on this sales slip.*

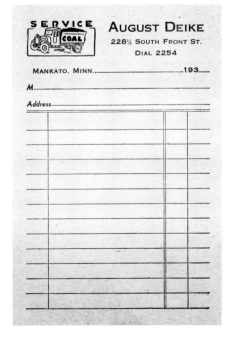

*Russ and Betty Deike, photographed on September 23, 1942, their wedding day.*

times chafed his father have been repealed. One result is that whereas Deike once had four major competitors, it has 54 today. Insurance rates have skyrocketed, and there was the imperativeness of continually updating his fleet, computerizing his record keeping, and modernizing his main Mankato terminal.

Jim Deike is most pleased by the loyalty of his employees and the number of awards received for safety.

August Deike Transfer, Inc., serves supermarkets, restaurants, retail stores, and factories, among oth-

ers. The most difficult assignment was transporting a massive metal sculpture, Paul Granlund's *Birth of Freedom,* from St. Peter to a church in Minneapolis.

Jim's wife, Christine, is vice-president of the company. They hope that at least one of their three daughters will carry on the century-old family business of August Deike Transfer, Inc., created by their great-great-grandfather.

# ACME CARBURETION

What Charles F. Butterworth envisioned in Mankato was a better strategic business location in Minnesota's agricultural heartland for his propane carburetion business. In the mid-1950s he moved what had been known as Magic Gas Service, Inc., from Ortonville and expanded its technical horizons under the new name of Acme Carburetion.

Magic Gas Service had principally been a distributor of propane for rural domestic cooking and seasonal home heating. But innovator Butterworth foresaw production year-round use for propane—an efficient alternative to pollution-laden gasoline and diesel motor fuels.

The energy crises of the 1970s found Acme Carburetion firmly implanted in Mankato and at the forefront of the alternative fuels revolution. Today Acme has become the Upper Midwest's oldest specialist in propane and natural gas carburetion sales, installation, and service.

Whereas propane-gas conver-

*Training sessions for propane carburetion mechanics are held regularly for dealers and other customers in Acme's large service area.*

*The late Charles F. Butterworth, founder of Acme Carburetion.*

sion of farm equipment was a primary objective of Acme in the 1960s and 1970s, the 1980s dictated that Acme respond to demands from fleet users to make their gasoline-driven vehicles more effective through installation of propane kits. About 80 percent of Acme's business is now wholesale to dealers, conversion centers, propane plants, and other industrial applications.

Diesel users, too, have benefited from Acme's business-oriented inventiveness. The Red Rooster Economizer is a device that injects a small amount of propane into a diesel engine to improve combustion, cleanliness, and economy. Acme added an electrical division in 1985 to fortify its repair and rebuilding abilities.

Donald Fettes, whom Butterworth encouraged to join the firm and who later became owner and president after incorporation in 1976, has followed and enhanced Butterworth's philosophy. Regular training sessions are conducted for fleet and garage mechanics, acknowledging that solid safety, installation, and troubleshooting practices are es-

sential for good conversions and satisfied customers.

"Although we are competitive within the industry," Fettes says, "we feel the extra service by our experienced employees is the prime reason for our growth. You can always buy a product cheaper, but you don't always get the help you need. There is no way to put a price tag on longer engine life, performance, or economy."

The legacy of C.F. Butterworth, recipient of the Minnesota LP Gas Association's highest achievement award in 1967, also lives on in more subtle ways. Not only was Butterworth a pioneer in gaseous fuel carburetion, but in 1960 he spurred development of a neglected industrial area of Mankato by relocating his plant there, situated on what today is identified as 110 Butterworth Street. His wife, Leila, once active in the firm, lives in retirement in Rochester, Minnesota.

# CLEAR WITH COMPUTERS, INC. (CWC)

For some years businesses have been employing the power of the computer to help them operate more effectively and profitably. However, computers typically had been used by businesses for budgeting, accounting, personnel matters, engineering, and manufacturing. But how about harnessing the computer for the neglected profit-center business areas of sales and employee training?

This thought raced through the mind of Jerry Johnson, a farm implement dealer in Elbow Lake, Minnesota, in 1983, when American agriculture was in a recession.

Johnson believed there should be graphics-enhanced computer software and readily available human expertise to better equip business employees, and to better inform their would-be customers. Ray Tuomala, a Mankato-based leasing manager and friend of Johnson, concurred.

As a result, Johnson and Tuomala became partners to refine what had been Johnson's computer-puttering hobby. Clear With Computers (CWC), one of Mankato's newest industries and among the latest in a

long line of home-brewed entrepreneurships, culminated from Johnson's unique idea.

What began as a two-man partnership, finding and exploiting a crack in the marketplace, has grown to more than 130 talented professionals and consultants operating out of three locations in Mankato.

It was appropriate that CWC's principal office would be situated in Union Square Business Center, a onetime elementary school and site of the first log cabin school in Mankato. The proximity to Mankato State University and Mankato Technical College proved to be a boon as well.

CWC's software and guidance permit large businesses to utilize the computer as a sales tool. The computer, perhaps portable, aids salespeople by organizing all the complicated, ever-changing information needed to maximize their sales efforts.

Say a client is an automobile dealer. A customer looking for a pickup truck wants to know the differences between the client's product and those of other dealers. The customer also naturally wants the "best buy" and the best options available. CWC-produced software can flash an immediate comparison on the monitor's screen, even a look at the

*Clear With Computers, Inc. (CWC), focuses on software to assist businesses and industries in training and sales efforts.*

dashboard makeup of the competing vehicles.

CWC's guiding principle was, and remains, salespeople—developing computerized sales and training programs for salespeople. The company's first agricultural client was International Harvester in 1983. Freightliner Corp., the firm's first nonagricultural customer, was added the following year. Today CWC serves numerous large corporations whose logos and emblems are among the most recognized in the nation, including General Motors, Case, Ford, and Kenworth. These organizations look to CWC to develop and support their training-sales computer systems.

CWC is admittedly not a business or industrial household name. This is because all of the CWC-created systems are custom packaged and individually marketed by the corporate clients to their sales staffs.

The firm is also international in scope. Overseas clients include Mercedes-Benz of Germany and Scania of Sweden. A French version of the software is available to clients in Canada, and three other languages are contemplated.

At present Clear With Computers has no known competition. It therefore expects more American and overseas businesses to visit Mankato.

*Ray Tuomala (left) and Jerry Johnson, founders of Clear With Computers, Inc. (CWC). Courtesy, Mankato Free Press*

# NORTHERN STATES POWER CO.

In 1989 Northern States Power Co. (NSP) noted 80 successful years in business. This public service octogenarian today uses conscientious energy management and advanced technology in behalf of 1.3 million electric customers and 335,000 natural-gas customers in Minnesota, Wisconsin, North Dakota, South Dakota, and Michigan's Upper Peninsula.

Among NSP's important consumer cities are Mankato and North Mankato, headquarters of the company's southeast region, the heart of Minnesota's agribusiness, a seat of learning, and an area of steady economic growth.

More than a century ago, not long after Thomas Edison invented the incandescent bulb in 1879, Mankatoans expected little from electricity. A single flickering gaslight was, to them, sufficient to illuminate a neighborhood. The iceman delivered ice in canvas bags from one nonelectric home to another. Coal and wood stoves kept most people warm and fed, but left a fine layer of ash on floors and furniture.

Lighting in Mankato was dim, dirty, or both. The choices were kerosene lamps, gas mantles, or an expensive 40-watt bulb. With electricity at 14 cents per kilowatt-hour, kerosene was definitely the better buy.

But low expectations soon soared. The idea of clean, powerful energy to help with the daily chores hooked the residents of the Upper Midwest. Stoic prairie townfolk, homemakers, railroad giants,

river-shipping magnates, lumber barons, millers, and quarry owners all were fascinated by the news that Edison had managed to illuminate lower Manhattan with the flip of a switch at his Pearl Street generating station in 1882.

Mankato Electric Light Co. was incorporated in 1885, later merging with the Mankato Gas Light Co. By 1900 the new entity was known as Mankato Gas and Electric Co.

Under the leadership of R.E. Brown, Mankato manager from 1889 to 1928, operations continued to grow. In 1910 Mankato Gas and Electric was acquired by Consumers Power Co. Until then, Mankato's electric utility was strictly local. But when the Rapidan Hydroelectric generating plant came on line in 1911, the nature of the business enlarged.

By 1914 Consumers Power was an interconnected system, thanks largely to Edison's protege and chief power-plant designer, Henry Marison Byllesby. He harnessed a small army of steam, hydro, and diesel plants and miles of shaky transmission lines and poles in four states. The system included Mankato and Faribault in Minnesota; Minot, North Dakota; Sioux Falls, South Dakota; and Fargo-Moorhead on the Minnesota/North Dakota border. In 1916 Byllesby's fragile grid of 25 properties became Northern States Power Co.

Today NSP, through able manage-

*William Maki (left), southeast regional general manager, and Gary Zimmerman, Mankato lineman foreman, examine an on-site application of cost-efficient underground service to customers.*

ment and advances in science, is doing what Byllesby struggled to do—bring dependable high-quality energy service to residential, commercial, and industrial customers, economically and efficiently. More than 100 years after the advent of the light bulb, NSP's prices are among the lowest in the nation.

NSP's long-term strategy is to continue high-quality service at the lowest-possible price by striving to manage power output levels (demand-side management) to the customer's advantage.

NSP works with residential, commercial, and industrial customers to change electric-use patterns to meet energy needs more cost effectively. It is a way to defer as long as possible the construction of new power plants while still providing an adequate and reliable supply of energy.

Through conservation and load management, NSP, since 1982, has trimmed peak usage nearly 250 megawatts from what the peak might have been, thereby reducing the need for constructing a medium-size power plant.

The Dotson Company foundry participates in NSP's peak-controlled rate by shutting down during peak use times and alternating the heating times of its two furnaces. This helps to lessen the peak electric load, especially in summer months when the demand is highest.

Bethany College's gym in Mankato changed lighting from incandescent to metal halide and fluorescent, thereby cutting demand and receiving a rebate from NSP. The Mankato public school system earned a similar rebate through efficient ballast and fluorescent lamps. Planners of Mankato State University's three-story computer center specifically selected lighting that not only qualified for rebate, but also helped save on annual energy expenses.

NSP's southeast region headquar-

*Don Schisel (left), NSP major account representative, and Hank Schollett, executive vice-president and chief operating officer of The Dotson Company, Inc., discuss peak controlling rates for Dotson's foundry in Mankato.*

ters in Mankato directs operations affecting 90,000 electric customers. The region is home to more than 200 electric utility employees, with about 60 at the Mankato Service Center. The southeast region is a 1987 cost-saving consolidation of two former operating divisions—Hiawatha, headquartered in Winona, and Keystone in Mankato.

Mankato's 24-hour dispatch center plays a key role. In addition to coordination, the facility responds to trouble calls from 26,500 NSP gas customers in Faribault, Northfield, Red Wing, Lake City, Wabasha, and Winona.

As a partner in progress with Mankato/North Mankato, NSP is an active participant in Valley Industrial Development Corp.—a grass-roots group organized to retain existing businesses and recruit new ones.

NSP participated with the City of Mankato in the 1989 purchase of 90 acres of land for a light industrial

park. The intention is to make the large plot available to manufacturers, printers, assembly operations, and others to provide quality jobs that balance land use and business development.

Another approach to economic development was a study backed by Northern States Power Co., Mankato's First Bank, and others that pinpoints what kinds of industry are best suited to southern Minnesota.

"NSP is committed to partnerships for progress," says Bill Maki, general manager of Northern States Power Co.'s southeast region. "After all, the greater Mankato area's future and NSP's are closely linked. We know it is in everyone's best interest to see that we continue to grow."

# MANKATO TECHNICAL COLLEGE

Why not expand the public education system to provide employment skills in the budding service industries for high-school juniors and seniors and returning military veterans?

This was the innovative proposition to the Minnesota Legislature, advanced by the Mankato School Board and superintendent J.E. Anderson in 1945. The concept was ac-

cepted, and Mankato was destined to be the first city in the state to have what then was called an area vocational/technical school.

A principal proponent was Harold Ostrem, who had joined the Mankato public-school faculty in 1939 to teach sales and marketing techniques. Under his direction, the high-school and adult curriculum began to include welding, electronics, and machine shop training to prepare a production line work force after America's entrance into World War II.

What today is Mankato Technical College held its first classes in 1947, following funding by the legislature, in rented midtown facilities that formerly had been Kline's, later Art Kost's, garage. This building, since demolished, was on the

*Mankato Technical College's three directors since its inception in the mid-1940s, from left: Harold Ostrem (1945-1949), Frank Kalin (1949-1976), and John Votca (1976-present).*

location now occupied by First Bank's auto teller and parking lot. There were three basic courses: auto mechanics, electronics, and machine shop.

Ostrem, in addition to his high-school duties, coordinated the program. Some of the early instructors were Ervin Treanor, welding; Harold Aga and Edward Steege, auto mechanics; Harold Mitchell and Ragnar Moen, machine shop; and John Dumont, John Gratner, and Charles Swanson, electronics.

When Ostrem left in 1949, first to be assistant vocational-education director for the state and then director of vocational and adult education for the City of St. Paul, Mankato's program was poised for dramatic expansion.

Ostrem's successor, Frank Kalin, helped to fulfill an Ostrem dream— a new facility adjacent to the modern public high school erected in what had been an inner-city slough.

Bond issues had assured its completion, and the vocational school opened in 1950, a year before the high school.

Kalin, like Ostrem, became one of Minnesota's outstanding vocational educators. He was a motivator and an innovator, championing and implementing trade apprenticeships, citizenship training, adult basic education, night classes, and, in general,

the opportunity for men and women to upgrade their job skills. He became president of several education groups and campaigned actively at state and national levels.

Kalin's inspiration was instrumental in the public's approval of a huge bond issue, resulting in a 200,000-square-foot independent campus in North Mankato, opened in 1968. By then, vocational training had been extended beyond the normal trade zone and the curriculum amplified further, to include practical nursing; secretarial and computer programs; graphic, commercial, and culinary arts; and sales and marketing techniques (Ostrem's forte).

Kalin was killed in 1976, when his car and a deer collided north of Mankato on his return from one of his innumerable night meetings promoting and expanding vocational education. John Votca was named his successor.

Votca, a Mankato native, had joined the school in 1955 as related training teacher and trade/industrial coordinator. He became Kalin's deputy in 1965, and, when at the helm himself, continued the advancement of occupational and job training. He directed construction of a 100,000-square-foot addition to the school that was dedicated in 1988. The new facilities included a teleconference center, bookstore, student lounge, library, an auto bodyshop department, and an additional classroom wing.

There had been changes in nomenclature, too, by legislative fiat through local initiative. In 1968 the school became known as Mankato Area Vocational Technical Institute. Ten years later, in 1987, it became, simply, Mankato Technical Institute and, in 1989, Mankato Technical College, with all programs converting to the course/credit system.

Throughout its 43 years Mankato Technical College's administration and staff have contributed significant leadership to education on state and international levels. They have been busy at home, too, with active participation in service clubs, Jaycees, Boy Scouts, Girl Scouts, Campfire Girls, and the chamber of commerce. It is the philosophy of the college to keep in tune with the public so as to provide quality technical education service.

Mankato Technical College remains, as it has been from the beginning, an arm of the Mankato District 77 Board of Education, under guidelines from the state.

As of July 1, 1989, the college had enrolled a total of 20,343 students over the decades.

*LEFT: The main entrance to Mankato Technical College. The twice-expanded, 300,000-square-foot facility was made possible by the generous contributions of Mankato taxpayers, the State of Minnesota, and talented faculty.*

*BELOW: The contemporary, sprawling campus of Mankato Technical College in North Mankato is a far cry from its humble beginnings in an abandoned garage downtown.*

# HUBBARD MILLING COMPANY

In the 1870s southern Minnesota was becoming one of the world's leading producers of spring wheat— a fact that had not escaped the attention of George M. Palmer and Rensselaer D. Hubbard, Mankato entrepreneurs. Palmer therefore proposed the idea of a new flour mill to Hubbard, and the two became partners in the Mankato Mill Co. (forerunner of Hubbard Milling Company), which was incorporated in 1878 and began processing wheat the following year.

Palmer and Hubbard were visionaries. They planned and built a steam-powered flour mill that would refine more wheat in one day than all the smaller mills in the outlying area could handle in one week.

They recognized that the railroads then serving Mankato would distribute flour to distant—primarily eastern—markets. No longer was the local homemaker their principal customer. Bakeries from Minneapolis to Chicago to New York City were within reach.

The mill was originally designed to use traditional millstones. How-

*George M. Palmer (1853-1939), cofounder of Hubbard Milling Co., challenged his employees with the words, "Make a [feed] concentrate that will make a profit for the man that feeds it."*

*Ogden Palmer Confer (1921-1988), Palmer's grandson and later Hubbard Milling Co.'s chief executive and a community activist, led the firm through its greatest diversification and expansion years.*

*The Hubbard Sunshine Minstrels performed on radio in the 1940s.*

ever, during construction a revolutionary new European technology was introduced. At great expense during a critical period, the mill was redesigned, and high-speed, gradual-reduction steel rollers were installed.

From the start the plant used a patented purifying device and therefore was able to put a high-grade product on the market immediately.

The company's leading retail brand, Mother Hubbard, and its commercial product, Hubbard's Superlative, became accepted as some of the best flour for home and bakery use.

From the beginning, Hubbard Milling Co. and Palmer and Hubbard themselves were integral members of the Mankato community. One of the

first three telephone circuits in Mankato linked Hubbard headquarters to city hall. Water from one of the firm's artesian wells was used to fight fires and clean streets. Until 1952 the mill's steam whistle marked the noon hour and the 9 p.m. curfew for children.

Hubbard died on August 30, 1905. The following year Palmer was elected president, a position he held until his death on April 18, 1939.

During his lifetime Palmer also served as president and chairman of the board of directors of First National Bank, president of the Baptist State Convention, mayor of Mankato, president of the Mankato YMCA, and a member of the Mankato Board of Education.

In 1928 the company began what would prove to be a long and profitable history of diversification, when it embarked on the manufacture of Hubbard's Sunshine All-Purpose Concentrates, nutritionally fortified high-quality livestock feed

to be blended by farmers with their own homegrown feed.

In 1946 Ogden P. Confer joined the business cofounded by his grandfather, George M. Palmer. Twelve years later he became president, then chairman of the board and chief executive officer. Under his leadership Hubbard Milling rapidly expanded and diversified its line of products. In 1946 the firm had a single flour mill and two feed-plant operations. Its sales volume that year was $8 million. Today Hubbard is multistate, very diversified, and a highly profitable business with annual sales of $250 million.

Through acquisitions, such as the Feed Division of Archer Daniels Midland in 1960, Vigorena Feeds in 1963, and Tri-State Milling Co. in 1970, Hubbard has expanded its animal-feed business. The firm has acquired a dozen feed-milling and grain-handling operations across the Midwest. A new animal-feed mill, constructed in Mankato in 1985, has received recognition throughout the industry as the most technologically advanced, computer-driven manufacturing facility for animal feed in the

*An artist's rendering of Hubbard's Mankato plant in 1928.*

United States.

Altura Rex Turkeys, Inc., of Altura, Minnesota, was acquired in 1964. It became Hubbard Foods, Inc., a fully integrated turkey-growing and -processing business.

Hubbard constructed a computerized pet-food manufacturing plant in Le Sueur, Minnesota, in 1982. With the acquisition of other pet-food companies nationwide, Hubbard has emerged as one of the largest producers of private-label pet food.

Today Hubbard has more than 30 manufacturing and sales facilities in the United States. The firm employs more than 1,300 people.

When Ogden P. Confer died on September 23, 1988, he had carried on the corporate record of service to his community and industry. He had served on the boards of the Mankato Old Town Development Corp., Active Community Thought (ACT), Mankato Area Foundation, Mankato Salvation Army,

Mankato Boy Scouts, Mankato YMCA, Leadership Mankato, Mankato Golf Club, Mankato Heart Health Program, Mankato Area Chamber of Commerce, and Minnesota Association of Commerce and Industry. He served on the board of directors of Norwest Bank, Mankato, from 1954 until his retirement in July 1988.

Confer received numerous awards such as the Mankato Exchange Club Book of Golden Deeds and an Alumni Achievement Award from Westminster College, Fulton, Missouri. He was inducted into the Minnesota Business Hall of Fame in 1984 and into the Mankato Area Business Hall of Fame in 1987.

The vision and enthusiasm evident when Hubbard Milling Co. was founded in 1878 has not waned. George M. Palmer's great-grandsons are now actively involved with the day-to-day operations of the firm. They believe the foundation laid by Palmer and their father, Ogden Palmer Confer, will be the base on which the company builds into the twenty-first century.

# AMERICAN BANKS

Mankato after the turn of the century was growing rapidly. European ethnic ties were still strong. A group of businessmen thought Mankato should have a banking establishment on the northern periphery of its major retailing district, and because the area was heavily populated by people of German heritage, it should be so identified.

The German American Bank was therefore founded in September 1906, Lawrence Henline being the prime mover. In addition to Henline, the first board of directors consisted of Joseph Stahl, W.C. Henlein, W.J. Morehart, J.A. Hielscher, Joseph Kroeger, and John Trenhauser. The original capitalization was $25,000 in stock.

There would be some stormy years ahead, but German American Bank immediately thrived alongside a burgeoning Mankato. Personal service to customers was emphasized.

German American survived President Franklin D. Roosevelt's "bank holiday" in 1933, following the debilitating stock market crash in 1929. The bank worked into the 1950s, redeeming losses experienced by its depositors during the Great Depression 20 years earlier.

The "German" identification caused some public nervousness during World War I. When unrest in Europe again developed in 1935, the word "German" was dropped, and the bank became known as American Bank.

American Bank has been at the same location since 1906, North Riverfront Drive and Plum Street. The original structure was removed in 1956, and its successor was dramatically overhauled and enlarged in 1978, an aesthetic improvement to what has become known as Mankato's "Old Town," complete with drive-in teller windows.

American Bank has had very stable management, with only five presidents in its 84-year history. Lawrence Henline served as chief executive officer until 1938. He was followed by Frank Darsow (to 1957), Ed Langes (to 1963), Erv Kurth (to 1983),

*The original American Bank building, shown here in the 1950s, was demolished in 1956 to make way for a new structure. The successive building was remodeled and enlarged in 1978. The bank has been at the same Riverfront Drive and Plum Street location since it was founded in 1906.*

and current chief executive officer Curt Zupfer.

From 1906 to 1963 stock in the locally owned bank was widely held. Then, Henry Henline, Jr., grandson of the first president, purchased controlling interest. In 1967 the late Ferdinand "Ferd" A. Buscher, president of the National Bank of Commerce farther down Front Street, struck out on his own and bought Henline's commanding interest.

The bank is now a part of American Bancshares of Mankato, Inc., a holding company owned by Buscher's son Robert, chairman, and grandson Bradley, president. Under Buscher ownership, American Bank has grown from $11 million in assets to $90 million, acquired facilities in Amboy and Lamberton, and been consistently profitable.

In addition to offering complete banking and financial services, American Banks operates the Prime Time Club, a unique group travel and entertainment network geared to thousands of its depositors over age 50.

*The late Ferd Buscher (center) brought American Bank into the modern financial world. His son, Robert (right), serves as chairman of American Bancshares, and his grandson, Brad (left), is president.*

# THE FREE PRESS

Moses Wickersham, a physician, had the prescription for Mankato businessmen clamoring for a newspaper in which to advertise their wares.

It was early 1857, five years after Mankato's founding. The townsite was expanding rapidly, and Wickersham knew of a printer back in Indiana who could be enticed to the Minnesota frontier.

What today is the *Free Press* had its origin in what became Clinton Hensley's weekly *Mankato Independent.* Hensley died in 1862, when he was reporting the Dakota Indian uprising. His survivors sold their interest to Charles Slocum, who renamed the newspaper *Union.* Still later, in 1880, the *Union* merged with a newcomer weekly, the *Record,* and the combined operation became known as the *Mankato Weekly Free Press.*

By 1887 Mankato was a full-fledged city, capable of sustaining a newspaper published every day but Sunday. Thus was born the *Mankato Daily Free Press.*

Solidly conservative in its political outlook, the *Free Press* soon had competition. Another weekly but passionately liberal paper, the *Review,* also went daily. Each paper worked spiritedly to win subscribers and to best serve the community's information, business, and social needs. Unification came in 1919, when the *Free Press* purchased the assets of the *Review.* Only the former's name survives.

The *Mankato Daily Free Press,* because of improved finances after removal of its rival, changed remarkably and soon became a stable newspaper in a burgeoning postfrontier environment. Better equipment; affiliation with the Associated Press state, national, and worldwide news agency; and introduction of pages devoted exclusively to sports, market reports, and comics combined to

*The staff and friends of the* Mankato Daily Free Press, *circa 1880, in front of the wooden-sidewalked office on Jackson Street at South Front Street. Executives are Frank Hunt, E.F. Searing (left foreground), and H.D. Fritz (left center, wearing suspenders), later president. Courtesy, Minnesota Historical Society*

give the Mankato area a complete newspaper.

In keeping with a new role as Mankato's single daily newspaper, *Free Press* editors toned down their partisan Republicanism and gradually assumed an essentially independent philosophy that continues to this day. "Daily" was removed from the newspaper's nameplate in the 1930s. In the 1970s "Mankato" was dropped by acknowledgment of the paper having become the printed ears and voice of many other communities.

The *Free Press* was privately held and operated by a succession of owners until 1979, when it was purchased by Ottaway Newspapers Inc., a division of Dow Jones and Co., Inc., New York. The modern plant is located in immediate proximity of the founding *Mankato Independent* of 1857. The *Free Press,* consistently at the technology forefront and recipient of numerous news-gathering and advertising awards, remains influential in local and state affairs, serving 26,000 subscribers in an 11-county area.

# KTOE

A group of businessmen holding the license to a would-be second radio station in Mankato had second thoughts about entering the broadcasting market. H.W. Linder, a pioneer broadcaster, stepped in to purchase their interests, and frequency 1420 on AM dials came alive in April 1950—more than 40 years ago.

KTOE is operated by Minnesota Valley Broadcasting, one of several Linder family entities in Minnesota and Iowa. Determined to be heard among south-central Minnesota airwaves, Linder devised an array of antennas that allowed KTOE's operation at a full 5,000 watts of power.

KTOE's first staff numbered 12 people. Linder's son, Don, station manager and vice-president, later became president. Willard "Bill" Smith, the only other original staffer still with the company, began as a salesman and announcer, later becoming manager. Another longtime employee is Rita Barten, who prepares daily programming schedules.

KTOE's programming reflects the Linder commitment to community service. In the early 1960s KTOE was the first area station to use mobile telephones for live remote broadcasts. Later the station was first to install satellite dishes for news and other programming.

KTOE's legacy of investigative news reporting personnel frequently made it first with the big story. Dur-

*KDOG's flashy Dogcatcher converted ambulance, seen outside the KTOE-KDOG studios, serves "Katoland's fun station" by bolstering the station's image.*

ing blizzards and tornadoes, KTOE was often the only station to remain on the air, thanks to its emergency generating equipment.

The station's semirural location on Highway 14 east of Mankato, however, forced its disc jockeys and newscasters to wait out the bad weather in the studios. Cots, blankets, and provisions are stored just for those inescapable events. Among the news directors who kept listeners especially informed were Wayne Will, Dick Lusk, Marc Tall, Jack Kolars, and, today, Jean Lundquist.

Sports coverage has been another KTOE forte. From 1950 to 1970 KTOE was the broadcaster of as many local sports events as any station in the state. "Ironman" play-by-play man Ben Dickmeyer—through today's Barry Wortel—followed teams throughout the large listening audience. KTOE was on the network of the onetime Minneapolis Lakers and, since 1986, has been southern Minnesota's voice of the Minnesota Twins.

KTOE's programming has changed with the times. In 1950 one could hear Don McNeil's "Breakfast Club," big-band music from the 1940s, polkas, and local insurance man Harold Ulvestad's recorded Swedish show on Sundays.

The menu began to change with disc jockey Slim Jimmy, who introduced his favorite country-western tunes. John Murphy lightened mornings in the 1960s and early 1970s with conversation and middle-of-the-road music. Hal Hoover appeared in the 1970s as a late-night jockey and Mankato's first genuine rock and roll announcer.

KTOE continues to flow with the winds of change. Today there is a variety of entertainment programming, from popular music to an evening talk radio program and Saturday's radio auction.

A sister station arrived on April Fool's Day, 1985. KDOG broadcasts at 96.7 FM, featuring adult-contemporary music designed by manager John Linder and the program director. It is known colloquially as "Katoland's fun station." Lip-sync contests, sailboat regattas, summer snowball fights, dances, and a garishly painted Dogcatcher converted ambulance have also been used to establish the station's identity.

The on-the-spot news side of broadcasting nonetheless remains foremost in the Linder philosophy of local broadcasting. KTOE reporters stood with sandbags as they fought floodwaters of 1951 and 1965, and at the side of fire fighters at the flame-engulfed Park Apartments. Announcers were at state tournaments to send play-by-play accounts of local athletic teams, and a news director was at the Main Street Bridge in 1970 to interview university students blocking traffic in protest to the Vietnam War.

# *MANKATO CITIZENS TELEPHONE COMPANY*

Connections have always been important to Mankatoans. From way back in the mid-1800s, when they supported the construction of railroads, telegraph facilities, and telephone lines, the city's residents have long recognized the value of maintaining contact with other municipalities and markets.

Mankato Citizens Telephone Company is one modern result of making good connections. Not only is the firm the prime telephone service provider in the area, it is also a vital force in several other areas of automated communications—from computerized digital switching to interrelated computer applications and fiber optics.

Mankato Citizens was founded in 1898 during a period when communications left much to be desired. At the time the area's only telephone company, the Northwestern Telephone Exchange Company, was providing poor service and charging ever-higher prices for it. When the utility could not be persuaded to improve service, Mankatoans decided

to call their own number.

As a first step, they embarked on a stock subscription drive to form a new telephone company. With new capital in hand, the fledgling utility erected its own lines in competition with Northwestern and halved subscriber rates to boot. Led by Judge Lorin Gray, Fred Kron, and John Meagher, the area's business people and farmers formed a urban-rural coalition that was soon making serious inroads into Northwestern's monopoly.

Within a year Mankato Citizens Telephone Company had 187 business and 87 residence telephones on line, linked by a switchboard on the second floor of the Brett Mercantile Building on Hickory Street. By the turn of the century the area's farmers—the most neglected population in terms of phone service—were part of the new Mankato Citizens network.

By 1901 a Mankato-based exchange had been established in Mapleton, to be followed in later years by exchanges in Eagle Lake, Madi-

son Lake, and Good Thunder. In 1909—little more than a decade after Mankato Citizens began operations—the utility had 2,008 phones in its communications web.

The telephone industry became subject to state regulation in 1915, mandating that one phone company be chosen as the prime operator in the area. Because subscribers to Mankato Citizens formed a majority of telephone customers, the state ruled that it would be the serving telephone company for the area.

Creation of Mankato Citizens was certainly a gamble, but innovation and expansion would continue to be the hallmark of the firm for the next 20 years. The company spent thousands of dollars pioneering service into the previously unreachable farmlands. A new headquarters building was constructed on South

*Mankato Citizens Telephone Company has come a long way since 1899, when this photograph was taken of the company's first switchboard. Manual operators and supervisors were required in the early days of telephone service.*

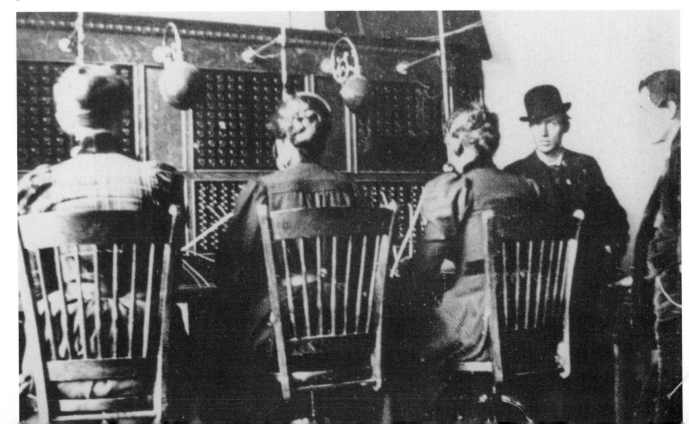

Second Street to house the firm's rapidly growing, service-oriented staff. In 1927 Mankato Citizens was one of the first independents in the country to institute automated dialing equipment.

Throughout these years P.M. Ferguson, Sr., who joined the utility in 1907 and ultimately became its president, was the company's foremost leader. His son, P.M. Jr., was also a major force in the organization in several executive and administrative capacities.

Though the Depression and World War II stymied expansion during the 1930s and 1940s, the company was ready to move again by the end of the latter decade. Adding sophisticated new equipment and a batch of new customers in Lake Crystal, Amboy, Vernon Center, and St. Clair, Mankato Citizens had 12,804 subscribers in 1952.

A special milestone for the organization was the 1965 acquisition of the area toll switchboard owned by Northwestern Bell. Direct-distance dialing and county toll-free calling were introduced and popularly received by the company's long-standing and loyal customers. All this was accomplished simultaneously with the construction of a modern plant and office building on Hickory Street.

Today Mankato Citizens has more than 26,000 access lines in the Mankato-North Mankato service area. Under the umbrella of Hickory Tech Corporation, the firm and related subsidiaries continue to pioneer use of state-of-the-art communications equipment: computers, fiber-optic cables, dig-

ital central office switching, and facsimile machines.

Midcommunications, Inc., one Hickory Tech subsidiary, serves telephone customers outside the Mankato/North Mankato area.

Computoservice, Inc., caters to the personalized computer record-keeping and payroll needs of a variety of business clients, from utilities to municipalities.

Information and Communications Services, Inc., sells and installs telephones, switchboards, voice mail, and message centers to businesses. It also operates Mankato Citizens

Econocall, a full-time long-distance service that is offered at lower rates than regular message long-distance.

Cable Network Inc. supplies television service to Good Thunder and Amboy. It also acts as the fiber-optic and electronic conduit between Mankato and Blue Earth-based telephone companies and AT&T's long-distance microwave transmission tower at Medford.

In the field of state-of-the-art telecommunications, Mankato Citizens Telephone Company has proved to be a smooth operator for almost a century.

_Mankato Citizens Telephone Company's handsome plant has dominated Hickory Street's landscape since 1963. The facade's huge, stone sculpture of a telephone lineman was carved by Paul J. Vetter, Sr., of Vetter Stone Co. of rural Mankato._

# HOLIDAY INN

For more than a century Front and Main streets have been the hub of Mankato's social, business, and hospitality activities.

Since 1979 there has been the Holiday Inn. Before that, there was the Saulpaugh Hotel, built in 1889 and demolished in February 1974.

The four-story Saulpaugh marked the city's transition from clapboard buildings and dirt streets to that of brick and pavement. The Holiday Inn also represents a benchmark in the downtown area's history—being a keystone in what was the community's second urban-renewal program.

In the 1890s the Saulpaugh's cavernous lobby and conference and dining rooms hosted travelers, conventioneers, and local revelers arriving by railroad and horse-drawn carriages. Today the Holiday Inn is continuing this tradition with all the modern amenities, serving guests driving automobiles or arriving by airplanes.

It is therefore fitting that the Holiday Inn stands on the site of the Saulpaugh Hotel. It was appropriate, too, that the Holiday Inn's main dining room was named "Saulpaugh" and that the adjoining lounge was named "Blazer," for the Saulpaugh's popular "Blue Blazer."

The Holiday Inn is owned and operated by DDD Motel Corp., a family business that was founded by the late Donald Anderson and his sons, Douglas and Dean. The idea was formulated by Douglas Anderson and then-Mayor Herb Mocol in September 1974 over coffee.

Since 1969 the Andersons have operated what today is the Garden Inn on Highway 169 in North Mankato. Urban renewal was dependent in part on a hospitality anchor for the proposed downtown mall. The Andersons considered a second facility in the heart of the Mankato area.

The Andersons recognized that Mankato/North Mankato was in great need of more lodging and hospitality space if Mankato was to regain its reputation as a convention center. Whereas two facilities in proximity could be a gamble, the Andersons seized the opportunity.

Feasibility studies proved favorable. And the potential problem of inadequate parking was resolved by the city government's erection of a parking ramp.

The Holiday Inn, with its 151 rooms, conference rooms, dining rooms, dance floors, lounge, and indoor spa, has been managed from the inception by Joe Leonard. Among his notable guests have been former President Ronald Reagan and former Vice-President Walter Mondale.

The new Minnesota Valley Regional Library is one of Holiday Inn's immediate neighbors, as are business and professional offices and the shopping mall. For history buffs, a dignified marker and sculpture depict events of the Sioux Indian uprising of 1862, brought to a climax just outside the walls of today's Holiday Inn.

*Holiday Inn's central lobby is Mankato's business and social gathering place.*

# *Patrons*

The following individuals, companies, and organizations have made a valuable commitment to the quality of this publication. Windsor Publications and the Mankato Area Chamber of Commerce gratefully acknowledge their participation in *At the Bend in the River: An Illustrated History of Mankato and North Mankato.*

Acme Carburetion*
Adamson Law Office

American Banks*
Clear With Computers, Inc. (CWC)*
August Deike Transfer, Inc.*
The Dotson Company*
The Free Press*
Holiday Inn*
Honeymead Products Company*
Hubbard Milling Company*
Johnson Fishing, Inc.*
KTOE*
Mankato Citizens Telephone Company*

Mankato State University*
Mankato Technical College*
Northern States Power Co.*
Regan, Regan & Meyer*

*Partners in Progress of *At the Bend in the River: An Illustrated History of Mankato and North Mankato.* The histories of these companies and organizations appear in Chapter 5, beginning on page 97.

*The farming industry in and around Mankato is dependent upon consistent yearly rains to ensure healthy harvests. Photo by Joe Miller*

# *Bibliography*

**MAIN SOURCES**

Apitz, Darrell F. *The Mankato-Kasota Limestone District: A Geographical and Historic Study.* Master's thesis, Mankato State College, 1963.

Bethany College. "Building for the Arts." Brochure published by the college, 1989.

Carley, Kenneth. *The Sioux Uprising of 1862.* 2nd ed. St Paul: The Minnesota Historical Society, 1976.

City of Mankato. *1988 Charter Anniversary Research.*

City of North Mankato. *The History of North Mankato: A Community Profile.* 1977.

DuBois, Cornelia Andrews. *Medical History of Blue Earth County, 1852-1902.* N.p., 1902.

Hughes, Thomas. *History of Blue Earth County.* Chicago: Middle West Publishing Company, 1906.

Lass, William E., Dr. *Minnesota: A Bicentennial History.* New York: W.W. Norton & Co., Inc., 1977.

Longwell, Chester R., Adolph Knopf, and Richard Flint. *Outlines of Physical Geology.* In *Outlines of Geology.* 2nd ed. New York: John Wiley & Sons, Inc., 1941.

Mankato. Board of Education.

Minutes for 1946-48.

*Mankato Free Press.* "Mankato Centennial Edition." 1952.

*Mankato: Its First Fifty Years, 1852-1902.* Prepared by the Semicentennial Committee for the 50th Anniversary of the Settlement of Mankato.

*Mankato-Kasota Stone Company—A Company History.* Published by the company, n.d.

*Mankato-North Mankato: Minnesota's Other Twin Cities.* Valley Industrial Corporation, 1989.

Mankato Technical College. *Annual Report,* 1987.

*Nichols Highlights,* February 1900. Chicago: George J. Love, Publisher.

Schellberg, Ruth. *History of Mankato Area Camp Fire.* N.p., 1988.

Schuchert, Charles, and Carl O. Dunbar. *Outlines of Historical Geology.* In *Outlines of Geology.* 2nd ed. New York: John Wiley & Sons, Inc., 1941.

Schwartz, George M., and George A. Thiel. *Minnesota Rocks and Waters. Revised ed.* Minneapolis: University of Minnesota Press, 1963.

**OTHER SOURCES**

ACT 2000 bulletins.

Blue Earth County Historical Society, archives and monthly newsletters.

Dotson Company, historic manuscripts.

Mankato Area Chamber of Commerce bulletins.

Mankato State University News Bureau.

*Minneapolis Corporate Report,* January 1987.

**INTERVIEWS**

Lowell Andreas
William Bassett
Sam Boruff
Frank Cesario
Ogden W. Confer
Dan Coughlan
Sylvan V. Crooker
Tom Gohla
Frank Hecht
J. Peder Kvamme
Fred Lutz, Jr.
Gertrude Meyer
Robert Ringhofer
John Rotunda
Glen Taylor
Willard Vetter

# Index